NE_Build & Grow

Get Ready to Read & Retell

1. What Is Retelling?

Retelling is the best after reading activity for young learners to summarize what they have read. Retelling helps readers create a mental image of the story. Also, retelling allows teachers to assess learners' comprehension as well as oral fluency.

2. What Is Oral Reading Fluency?

Oral reading fluency is the ability to read a text with accuracy, good speed, and good expression. Oral reading fluency activities help boost oral competency and also their understanding.

Oral Reading Fluency

Fluent readers can read a story with **accuracy**, **good speed**, and **good expression**.

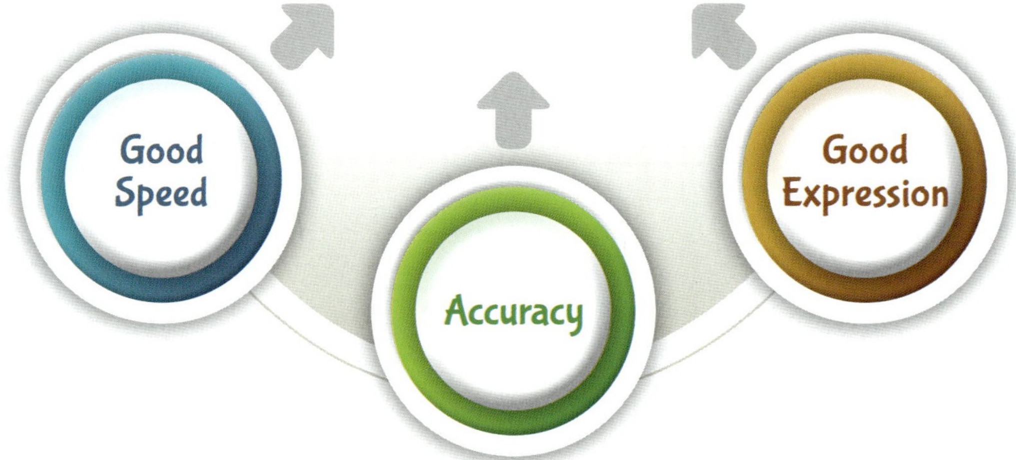

Tour of Read & Retell

Before Reading

Words

New words are introduced with pictures and help learners get ready for the story.

Before You Read

A quick and simple activity helps learners actively explore the picture, and predict the story before reading it.

While Reading

Read for Oral Reading Fluency

An engaging story is presented, and a dynamic oral activity helps learners build their oral reading fluency.

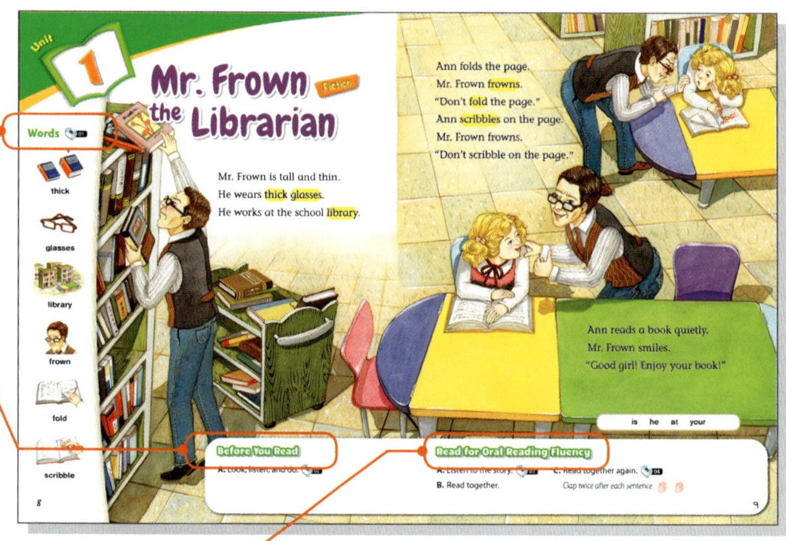

After Reading

Retell

A guided retelling activity provides an opportunity for learners to recall and process the story, and to retell the story to others.

Comprehension

Comprehension questions confirm learners' understanding of the story.

Literacy Center

Brief examples of the pronunciation, grammar, high frequency words, and punctuation from the story reinforce learners' literacy.

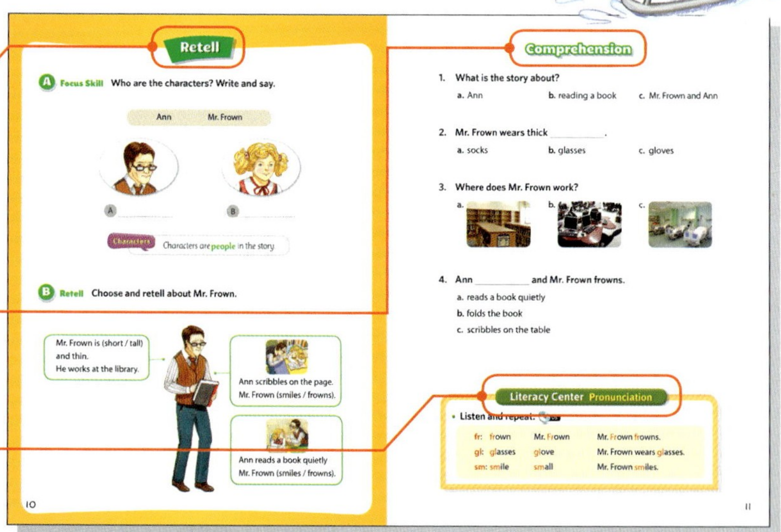

Reading Day
Retelling Day

Read & Retell special section includes two units; Reading Day and Retelling Day. These units enable learners to prepare and present their retelling with a uniquely designed, removable retelling chart.

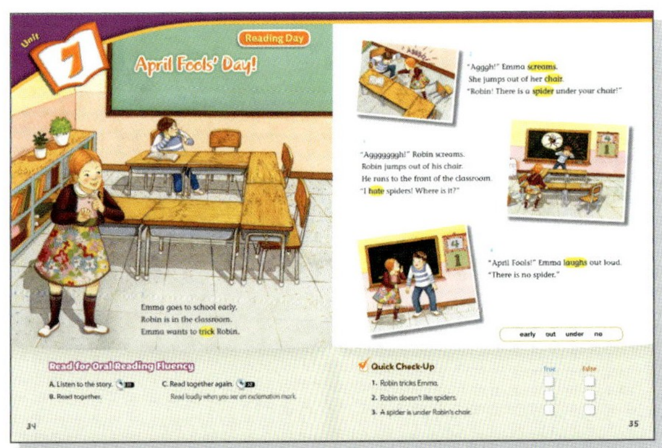

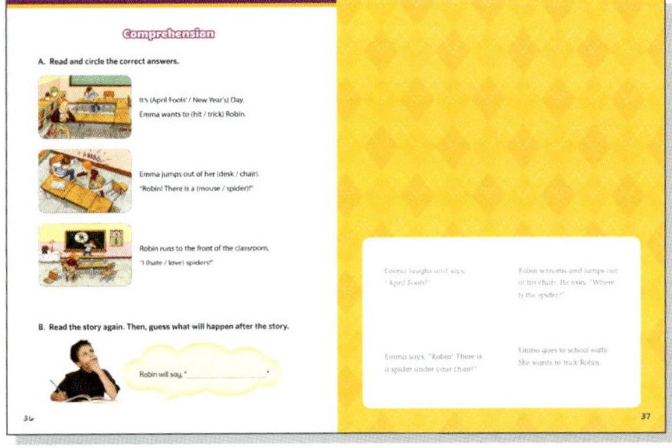

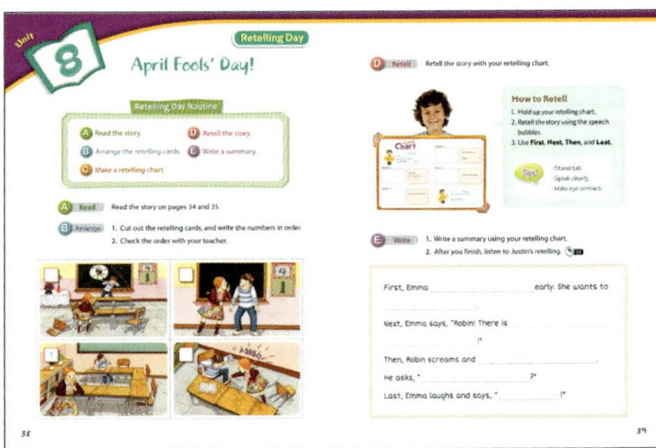

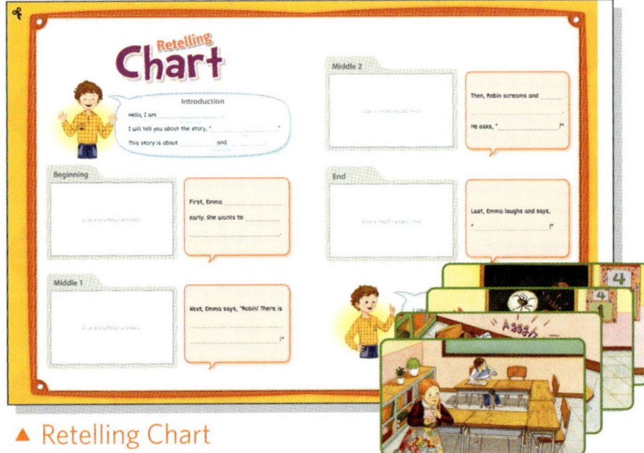

▲ Retelling Chart

▲ Retelling Cards

Contents

Mr. Frown the Librarian

Fiction

Words  01

thick

glasses

library

frown

fold

scribble

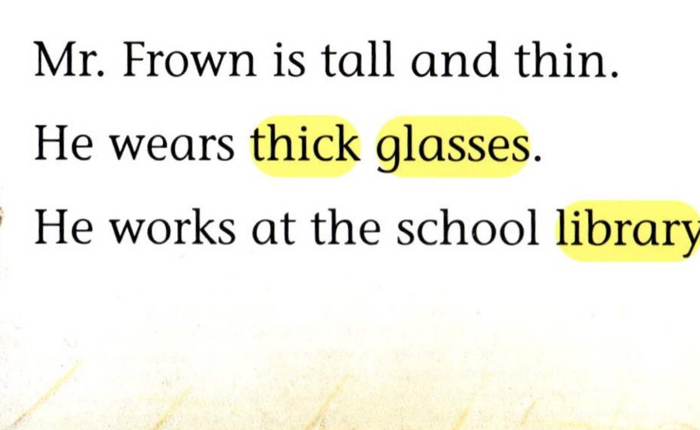

Mr. Frown is tall and thin.
He wears thick glasses.
He works at the school library.

Before You Read

A. Look, listen, and do.  02

Read for Oral Reading Fluency

A. Listen to the story. 03

B. Read together.

C. Read together again. 04

Clap twice after each sentence.

A **Focus Skill** Who are the characters? Write and say.

Ann   Mr. Frown

A ___________________   B ___________________

Characters Characters are **people** in the story.

B **Retell** Choose and retell about Mr. Frown.

Comprehension

1. **What is the story about?**

   a. Ann   **b.** reading a book   **c.** Mr. Frown and Ann

2. **Mr. Frown wears thick ___________.**

   a. socks   **b.** glasses   **c.** gloves

3. **Where does Mr. Frown work?**

   a.    **b.**    **c.** 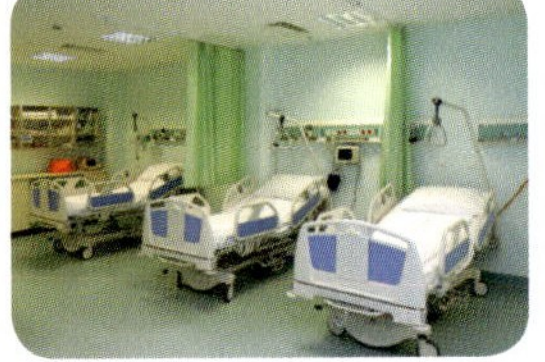

4. **Ann ___________ and Mr. Frown frowns.**

   a. reads a book quietly

   b. folds the book

   c. scribbles on the table

Literacy Center Pronunciation

- **Listen and repeat.**  05

fr: frown	Mr. Frown	Mr. Frown frowns.
gl: glasses	glove	Mr. Frown wears glasses.
sm: smile	small	Mr. Frown smiles.

Unit 2

Let's Play!

Fiction

Words 06

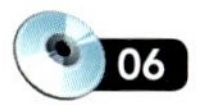

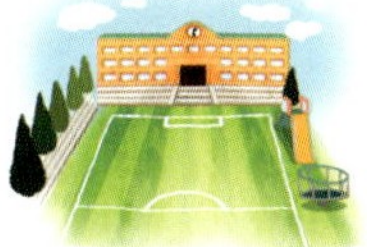

playground

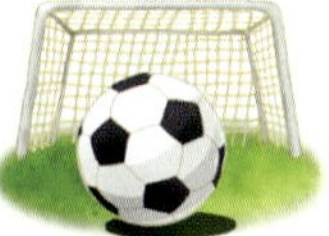

soccer

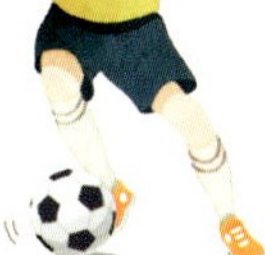

dribble

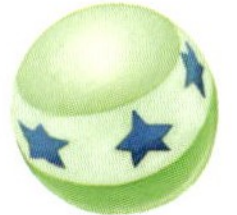

ball

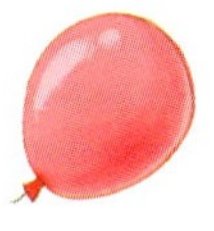

balloon

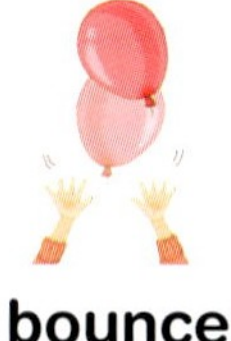

bounce

Bill, Sam, and Tina are at the playground.
"What shall we play?" says Bill.
"Let's play soccer," says Sam.
He dribbles the ball.

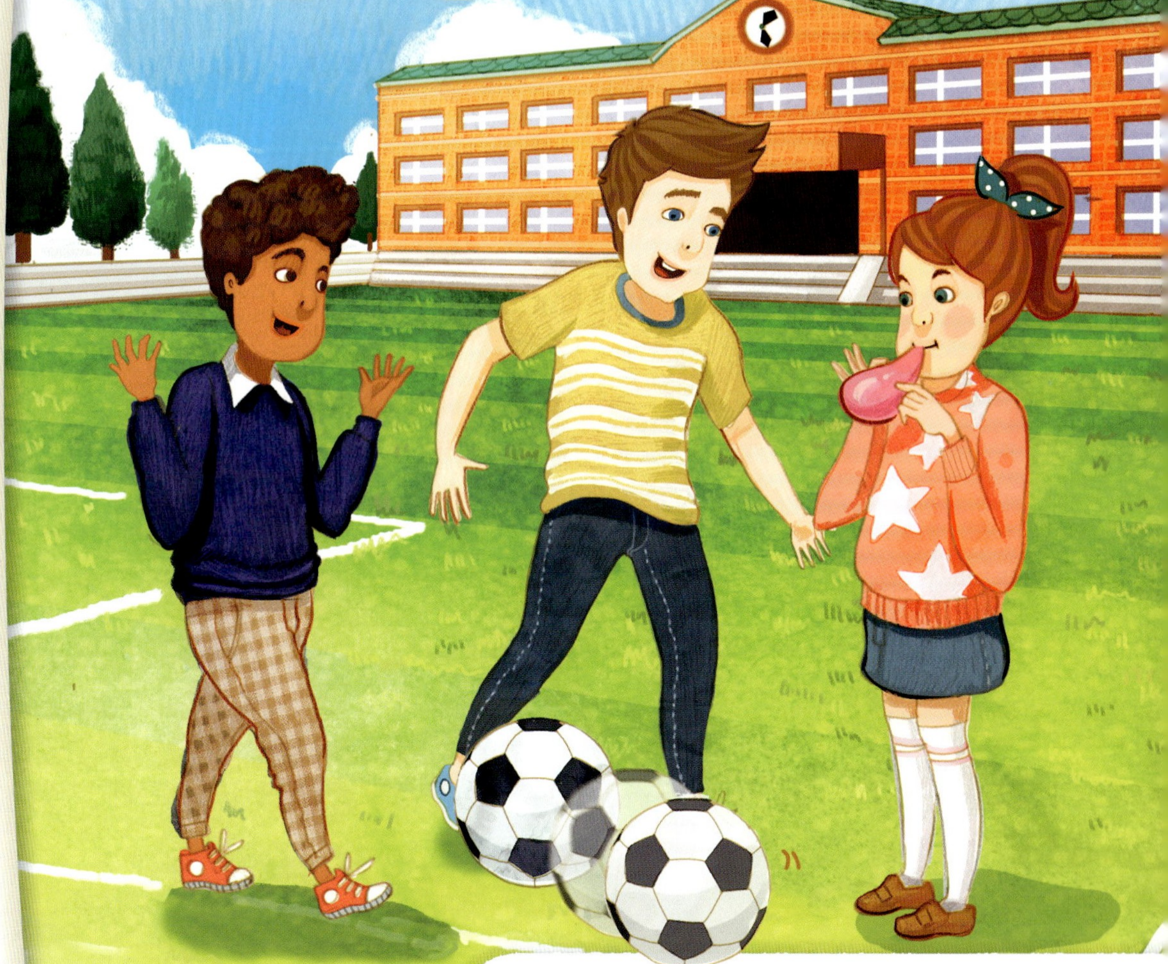

Before You Read

A. Look, listen, and do. 07

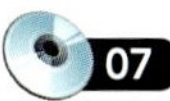

"No, let's play with a balloon,"
says Tina.
She bounces the balloon.

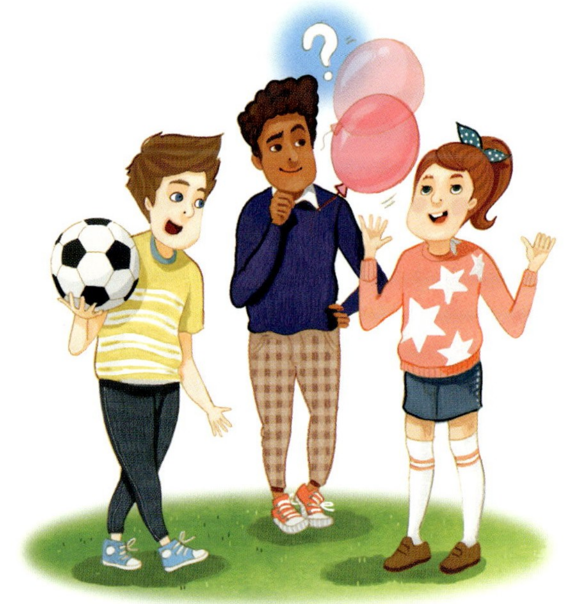

"Aha! Let's play balloon soccer!" says Bill.
"That sounds fun," say Sam and Tina.
They play together happily.

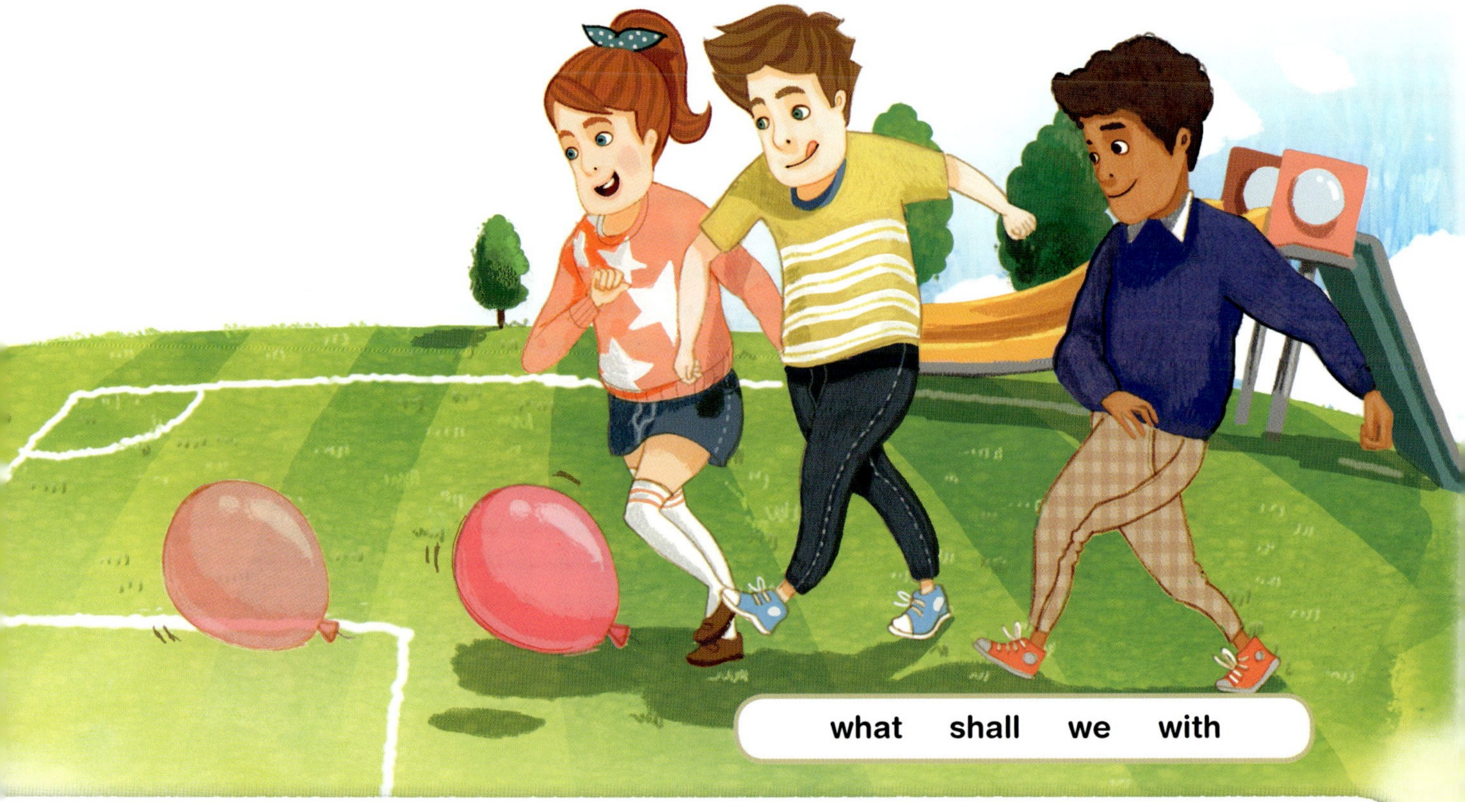

what shall we with

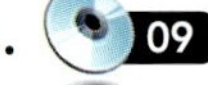

Read for Oral Reading Fluency

A. Listen to the story. 08

B. Read together.

C. Read together again. 09

Use different voices for each character.

Retell

A **Focus Skill**   What do the characters say? Write and act out.

balloon   soccer   balloon soccer

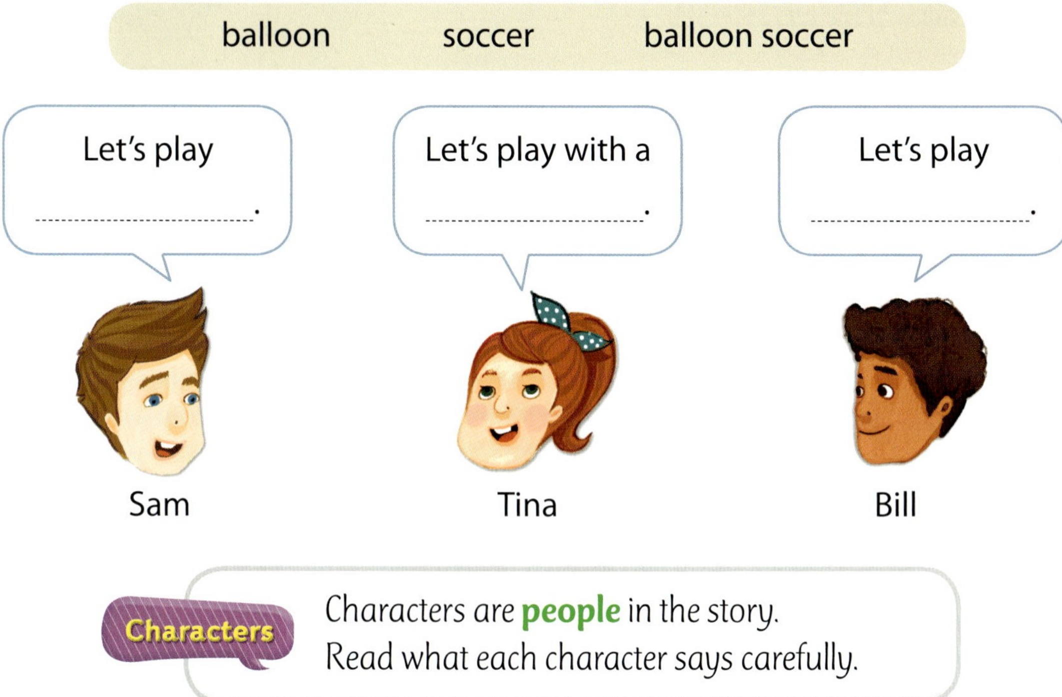

Characters   Characters are **people** in the story.
Read what each character says carefully.

B **Retell**   Read and number in order. Retell the story to your partner.

Tina wants to play with a balloon.

Sam wants to play soccer.

They play balloon soccer together.

First → Next → Then

Comprehension

1. What is the story about?

    a. studying together

    b. playing together

    c. reading together

2. Where are Bill, Sam, and Tina?

    a. at the gym   **b.** at the park   **c.** at the playground

3. Sam __________ the ball.

    a. dribbles

    b. bounces

    c. catches

4. __________ wants to play with a balloon.

    a. Bill   **b.** Sam   **c.** Tina

Literacy Center Grammar

- **Listen and repeat.**  10

Let's play soccer.	Let's dribble the ball.
Let's bounce the ball.	Let's read a book.

Unit 3

Places at School

Nonfiction

Words (11)

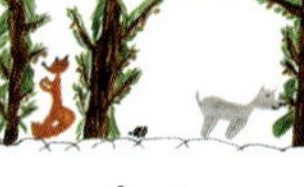

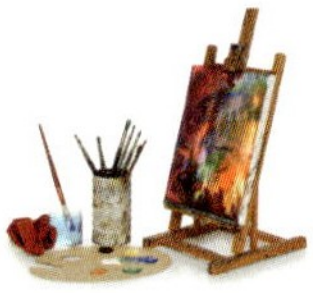
art

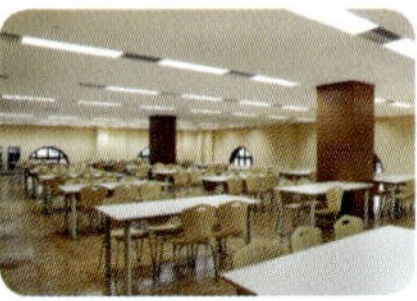

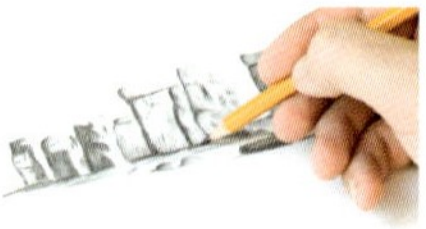
draw

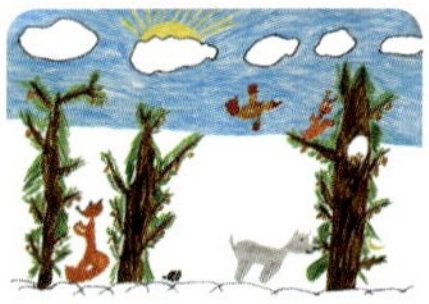

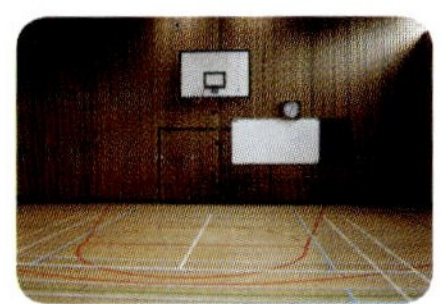

picture

cafeteria

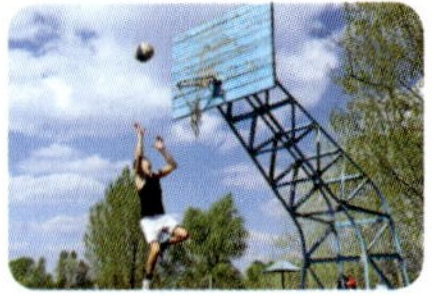

gym

basketball

There are many places at school.

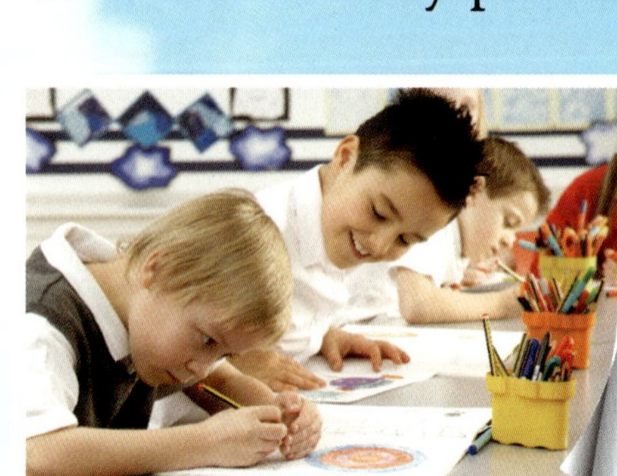

Where are the students?
They are in the art room.
They draw pictures
in the art room.

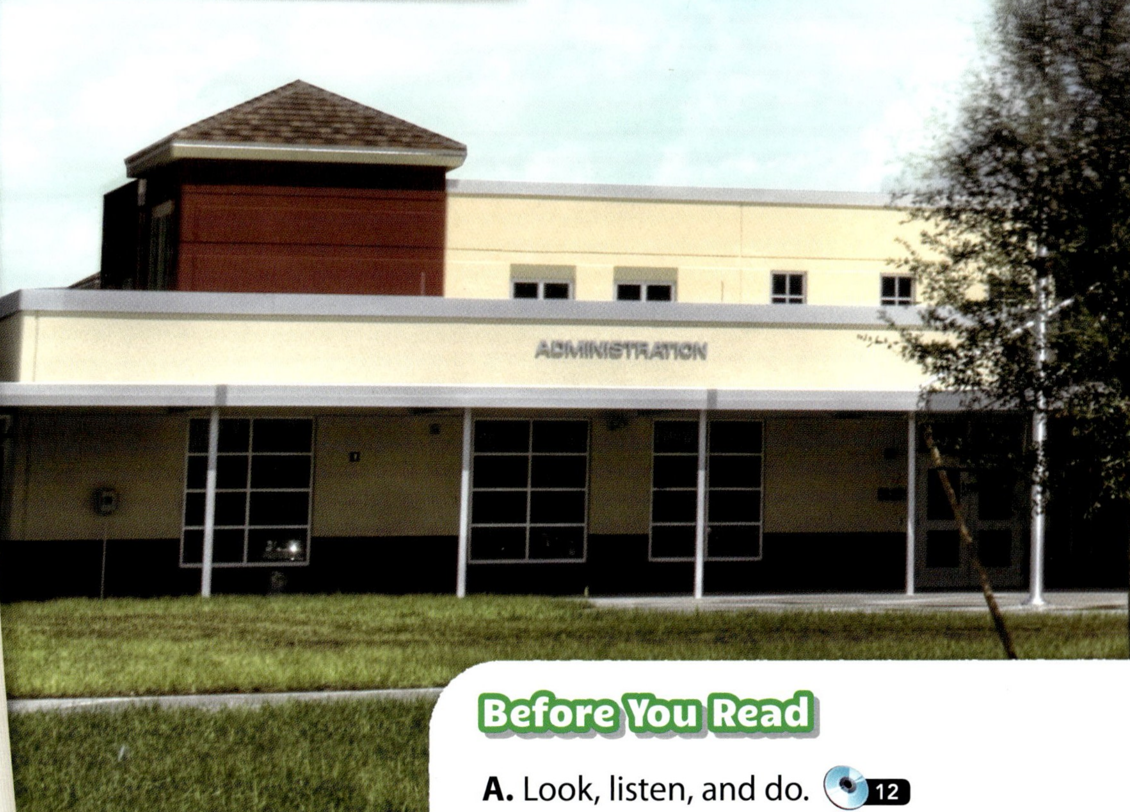

Before You Read

A. Look, listen, and do. (12)

Where are they?

They are in the cafeteria.

They have a delicious lunch
in the cafeteria.

Where are they?

They are in the gym.

They play basketball in the gym.

are   the   they   in

Read for Oral Reading Fluency

A. Listen to the story. `13`

B. Read together.

C. Read together again. `14`

They are **in** the (**art room**).

17

Retell

A **Focus Skill** Look at the main idea and details of the story.

Main idea

Details

The main idea is the **big idea** in the story.
Details **tell more** about the main idea.

B **Retell** Write and retell about the places at school.

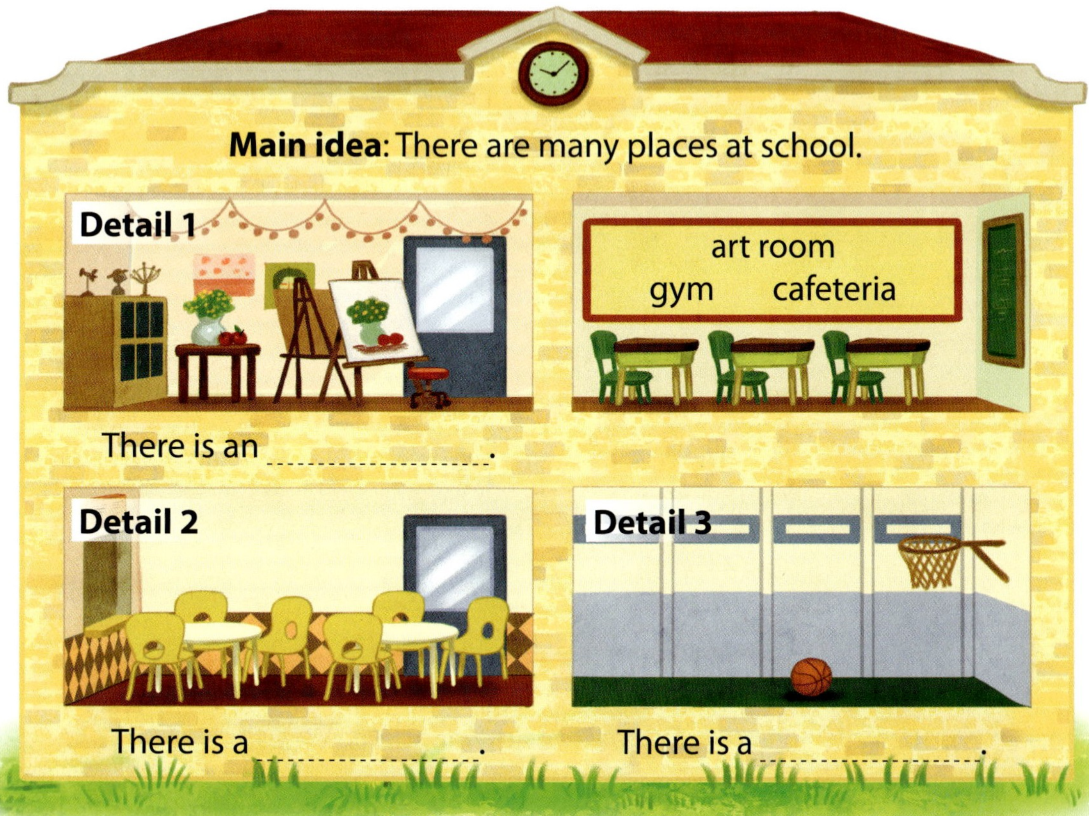

Comprehension

1. **What is the story about?**

   a. students at school   **b.** places at school   **c.** school uniforms

2. **The students draw pictures in the ____________.**

   a. art room   **b.** playground   **c.** classroom

3. **The students have ____________ in the cafeteria.**

   a. snacks   **b.** lunch   **c.** breakfast

4. **Where do the students play basketball?**

   a.    **b.**    **c.** 

Friday Music Class

Fiction

perform

worried

nervous

stand

cheer

proud

Today is Friday.

It's art class.

My music class is soon!

I have to perform a song in music class.

Yikes! I feel worried.

Before You Read

A. Look, listen, and do.  16

It's lunchtime.
My music class is after lunch!
Gulp! I feel nervous.

Finally, it's music class!
I stand tall and sing loudly.
La, la, la ⋯.
Everyone claps and cheers.
Phew! I feel proud.

| my | soon | have | after |

Read for Oral Reading Fluency

A. Listen to the story.  17

C. Read together again.  18

B. Read together.

Use your voice to show how the character feels.

A **Focus Skill** When does this story happen? Choose and say.

Time The time is **when** the story happens.

B **Retell** Write and retell about the Friday music class.

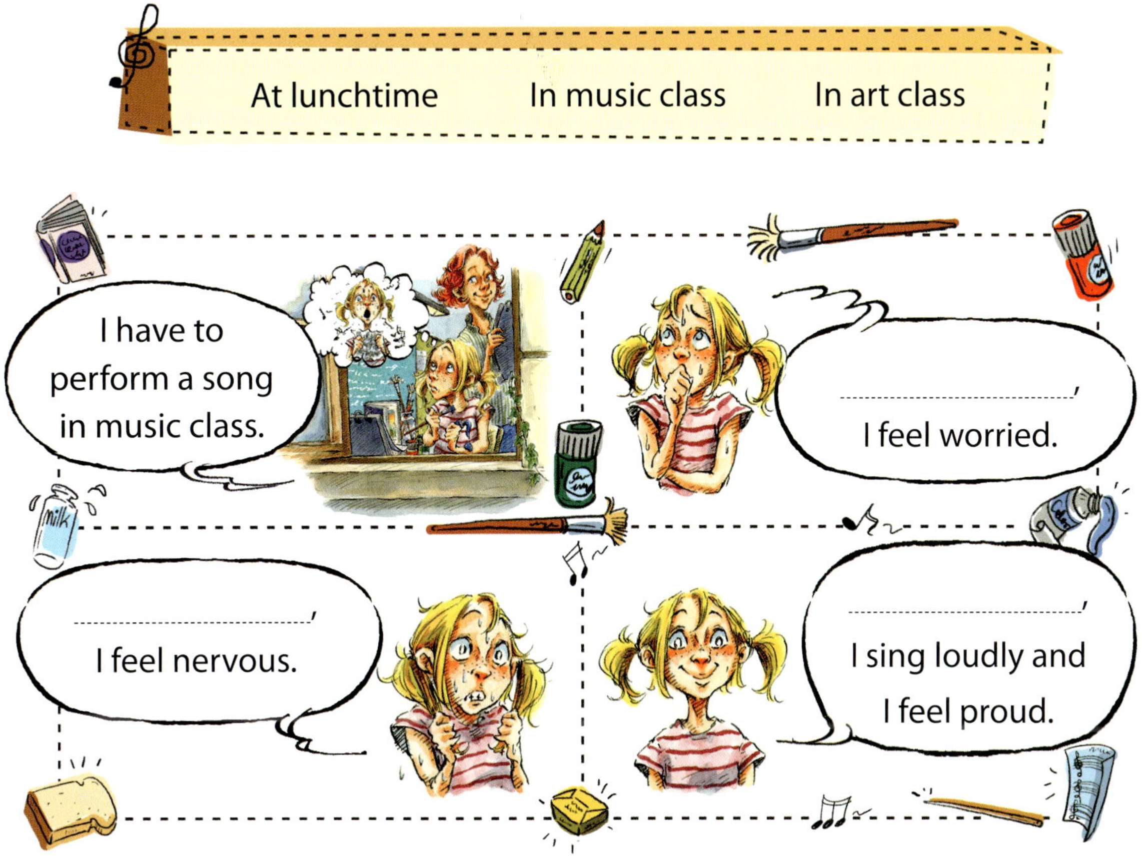

Comprehension

1. **What is the story about?**

    a. drawing a picture

    b. performing a song

    c. eating lunch

2. **In _____________ class, the girl feels worried.**

    a. art   **b.** music   **c.** math

3. **The girl stands tall and sings _____________.**

    a. softly   **b.** loudly   **c.** quietly

4. **How does the girl feel at the end of the story?**

    a.    **b.**    **c.** 

Literacy Center Pronunciation

- **Listen and repeat.**  19

  short vowel a: apple   cat   rat   ham

  clap   class   stand   after

  A cat and a rat stand and clap.

Unit 5

Henry Hurry Hurries

Fiction

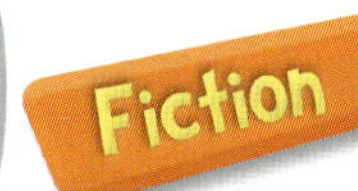

Words

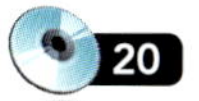

20

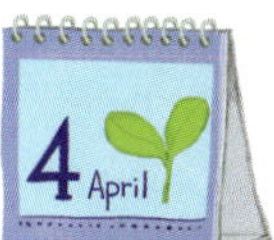

April

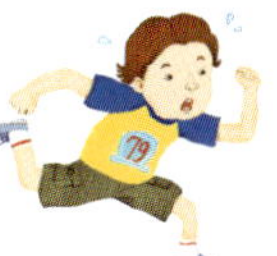

hurry

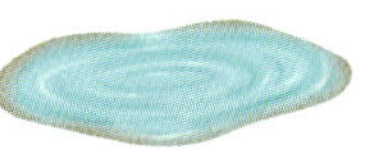

puddle

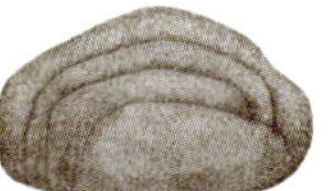

rock

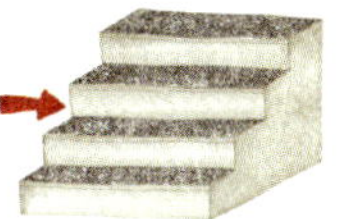

stair

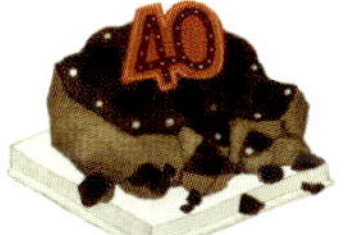

messy

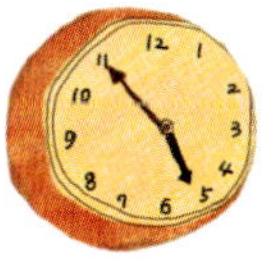

Henry Hurry buys a chocolate cake.

It is the fifth of April.

It is his mother's fortieth birthday.

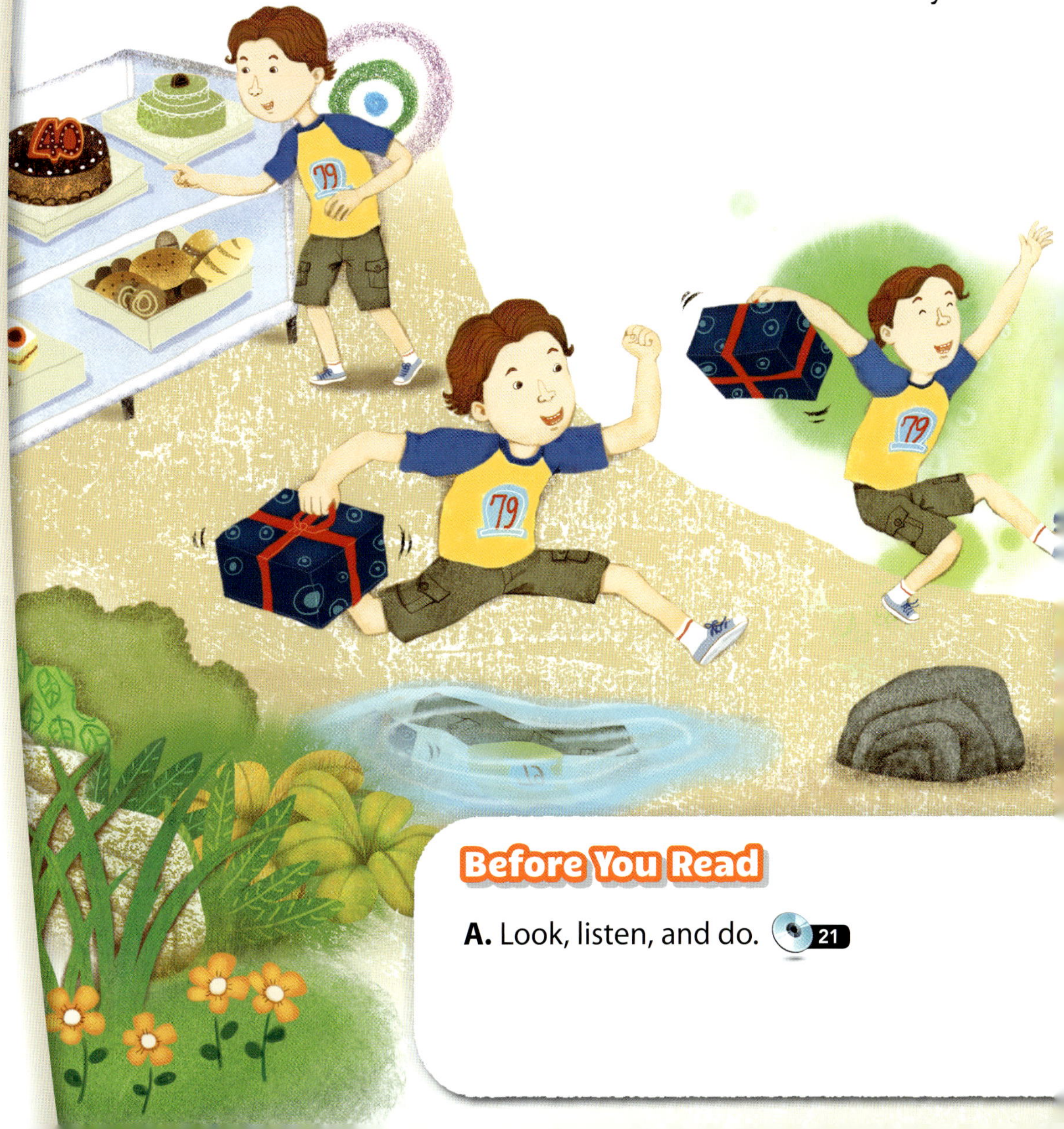

Before You Read

A. Look, listen, and do. 21

Henry Hurry **hurries** to his house.
He jumps over the **puddle**.
He jumps over the **rock**.
He jumps up the **stairs**.

Henry Hurry opens the cake box.
Uh-oh! The chocolate cake is **messy**.
His mother says, "It is messy but
still sweet."

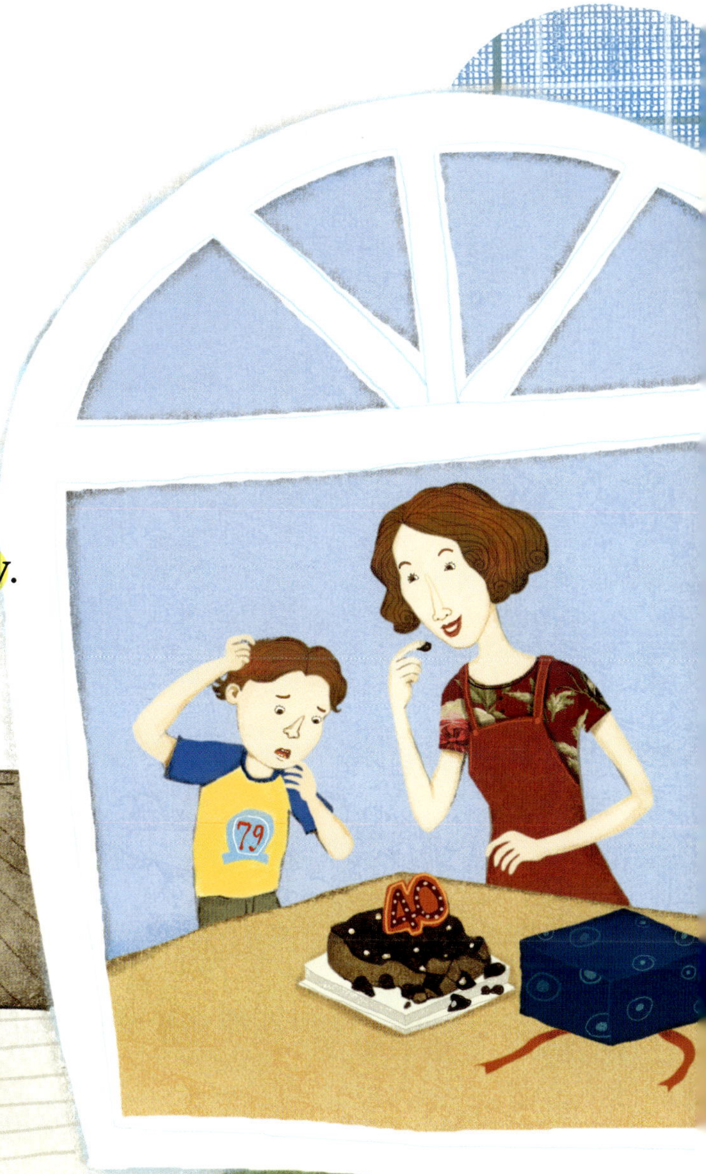

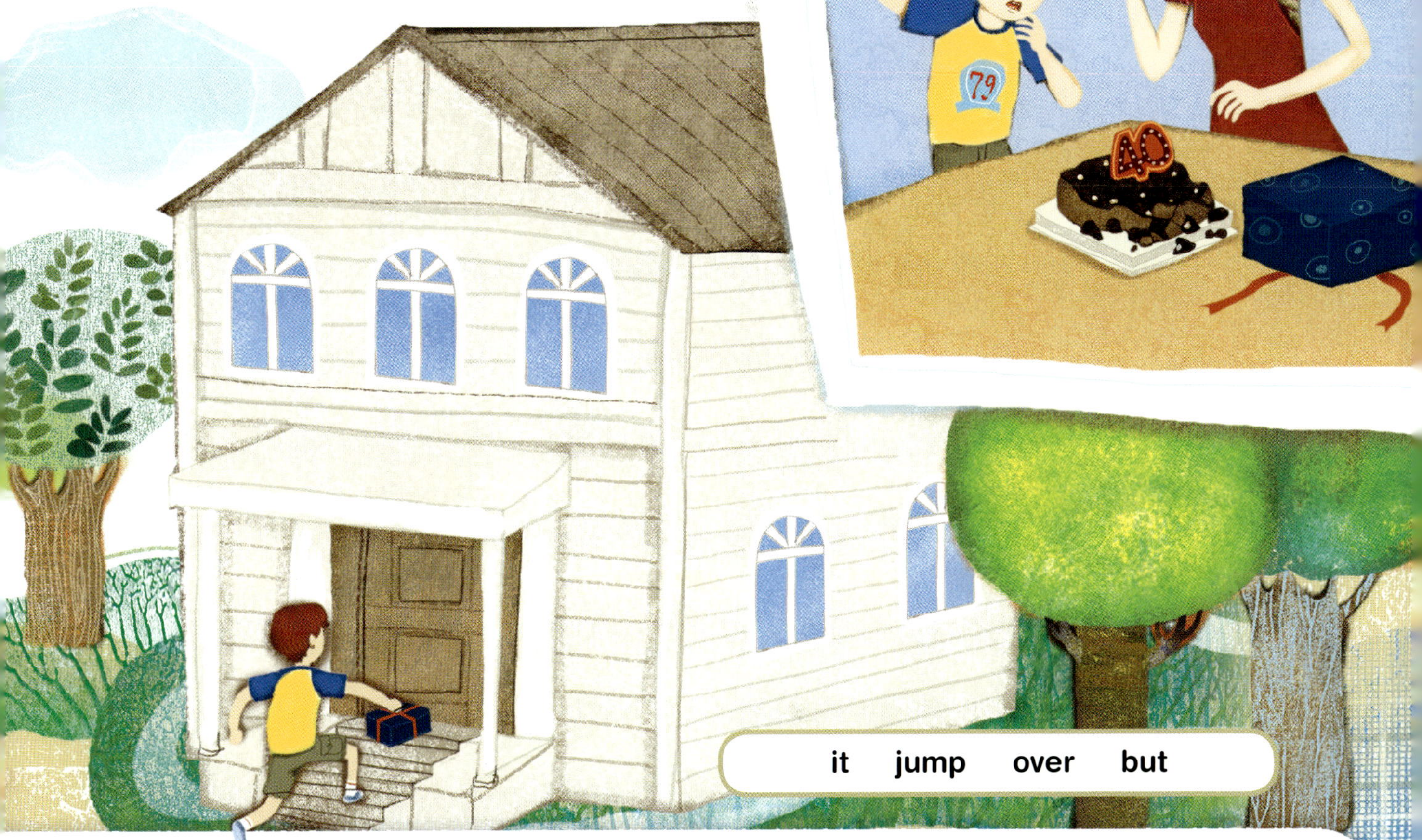

Read for Oral Reading Fluency

A. Listen to the story.  22

C. Read together again. 23

B. Read together.

He jumps (**over** the **puddle**).

Retell

Focus Skill   **When is Henry Hurry's mother's birthday? Write and say.**

April   August   fifth   fourth

Time   The time is **when** the story happens.

Retell   **Read and number in order. Retell the story to your partner.**

He opens the cake box. The chocolate cake is messy. But his mom likes it.

Henry Hurry hurries to his house.

Henry Hurry buys a chocolate cake for his mother.

Tip!   First → Next → Then

26

Comprehension

1. **What is the story about?**

   a. a chocolate cake

   b. Henry Hurry's birthday

   c. Henry Hurry's mother's birthday

2. **Henry Hurry's mother is ____________ years old.**

   a. fourteen   **b.** forty   **c.** forty five

3. **What does Henry Hurry jump over?**

   a.    **b.**    **c.** 

4. **Henry Hurry's mother thinks the cake is ____________ but sweet.**

   a. big   **b.** messy   **c.** pretty

Literacy Center Grammar

- **Listen and repeat.**  24

four - fourth	five - fifth	six - sixth
seven - seventh	eight - eighth	nine - ninth

6

Good Snacks and Bad Snacks

Nonfiction

Words  25

vegetable

full

healthy

fast food

soda

unhealthy

There are many snacks around us.
Some snacks are good for us.
Some snacks are bad for us.

Before You Read

A. Look, listen, and do. 26

Fruits and **vegetables** are good for us.

They are **full** of vitamins and minerals.

They make us **healthy**.

Fast food, sweets, and **soda** are bad for us.

They are full of sugar and salt.

They make us **unhealthy**.

29

Retell

A Focus Skill   What is the main idea?

Main Idea & Details   The main idea is the **big idea** in the story. Details **tell more** about the main idea.

B Retell   Write and retell about the good snacks and bad snacks.

Main idea   Some snacks are good, and some snacks are bad.

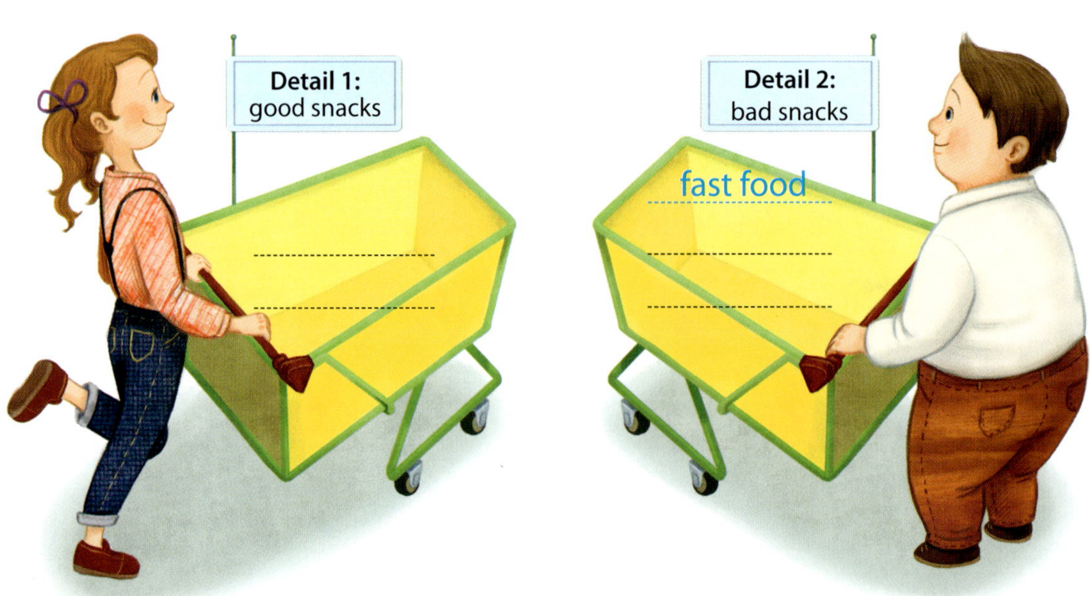

30

Comprehension

1. **What is the story about?**

   a. fast food

   b. good snacks and bad snacks

   c. sugar and salt

2. **Which snack is good for us?**

   a.    b.    c. 

3. **Vegetables are full of ____________.**

   a. salt   **b.** sugar   **c.** vitamins

4. **Too much sugar and salt make us ____________.**

   a. healthy   **b.** strong   **c.** unhealthy

Literacy Center High Frequency Words

- **Listen and circle the same words. Then count them.**  29

1. **and**	ant	and	an	and	(	)
2. **for**	four	for	fox	fur	(	)
3. **full**	fall	full	full	pull	(	)

Read & Retell 1

April Fools' Day!

Unit 7 — Reading Day

We will read a story about Emma and Robin.
Emma wants to trick Robin.

Unit 8 — Retelling Day

We will retell the story, "April Fools' Day!"

Words

Listen and repeat.  30

trick

scream

chair

spider

hate

laugh

Before You Read

Picture Ⓐ What is the boy looking for?

Picture Ⓑ Guess why the girl laughs.

April Fools' Day!

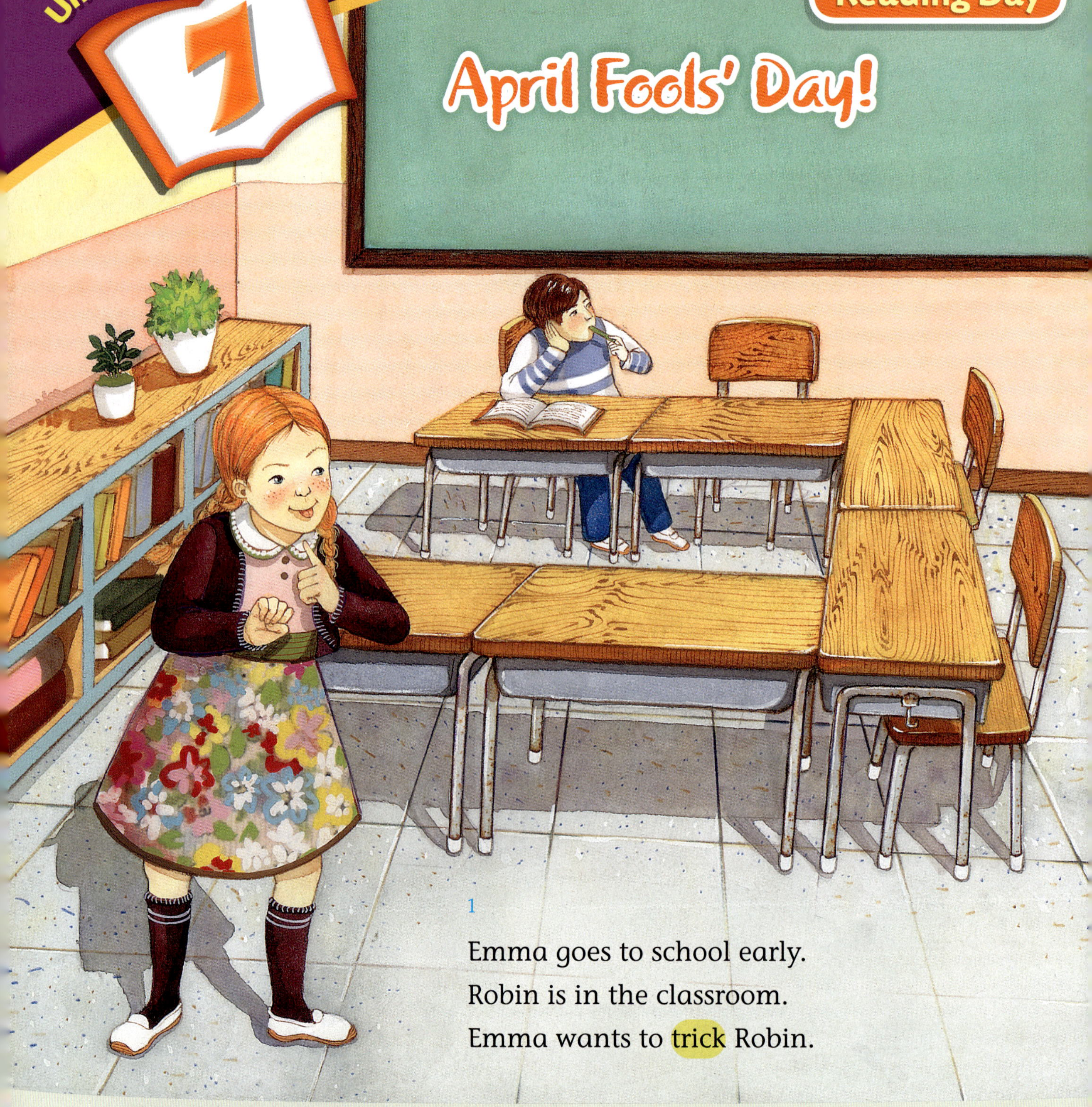

1

Emma goes to school early.
Robin is in the classroom.
Emma wants to **trick** Robin.

Read for Oral Reading Fluency

A. Listen to the story. 

B. Read together.

C. Read together again. 

Read loudly when you see an exclamation mark.

2

"Agggh!" Emma screams.
She jumps out of her chair.
"Robin! There is a spider under your chair!"

3

"Aggggggggh!" Robin screams.
Robin jumps out of his chair.
He runs to the front of the classroom.
"I hate spiders! Where is it?"

4

"April Fools!" Emma laughs out loud.
"There is no spider."

early	out	under	no

✓ **Quick Check-Up**

	True	False
1. Robin tricks Emma.	☐	☐
2. Robin doesn't like spiders.	☐	☐
3. A spider is under Robin's chair.	☐	☐

Comprehension

A. Read and circle the correct answers.

It's (April Fools' / New Year's) Day.

Emma wants to (hit / trick) Robin.

Emma jumps out of her (desk / chair).

"Robin! There is a (mouse / spider)!"

Robin runs to the front of the classroom.

"I (hate / love) spiders!"

B. Read the story again. Then, guess what will happen after the story.

Robin will say, "______________________________."

Emma laughs and says,
"April Fools!"

Robin screams and jumps out
of his chair. He asks, "Where
is the spider?"

Emma says, "Robin! There is
a spider under your chair!"

Emma goes to school early.
She wants to trick Robin.

April Fools' Day!

Retelling Day Routine

- **A** Read the story.
- **B** Arrange the retelling cards.
- **C** Make a retelling chart.
- **D** Retell the story.
- **E** Write a summary.

A Read — Read the story on pages 34 and 35.

B Arrange
1. Cut out the retelling cards, and write the numbers in order.
2. Check the order with your teacher.

Retelling Chart 1

C Make

1. Complete the **red** speech bubbles. (Hints are at the back of the cards.)
2. **Glue** the retelling cards.
3. Complete the **blue** speech bubbles.

name

¡Agggh!

D Retell   Retell the story with your retelling chart.

How to Retell

1. Hold up your retelling chart.
2. Retell the story using the speech bubbles.
3. Use **First**, **Next**, **Then**, and **Last**.

Tips!
- Stand tall.
- Speak clearly.
- Make eye contact.

E Write   1. Write a summary using your retelling chart.

2. After you finish, listen to Justin's retelling. 

First, Emma ___________________________ early. She wants to

___________________________.

Next, Emma says, "Robin! There is ___________________________

___________________________!"

Then, Robin screams and ___________________________.

He asks, "___________________________?"

Last, Emma laughs and says, "___________________________!"

We Live in the Antarctic

Fiction

Words 34

krill

Antarctic

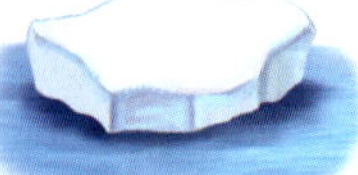

ice

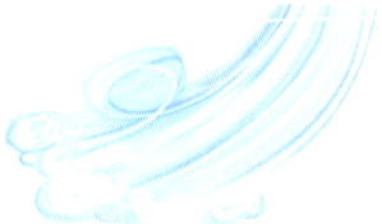

wind

volcano

sled

Hi! I'm Penguin.

These are my friends, Whale, Seal, and Krill.

We live in the Antarctic, around the South Pole.

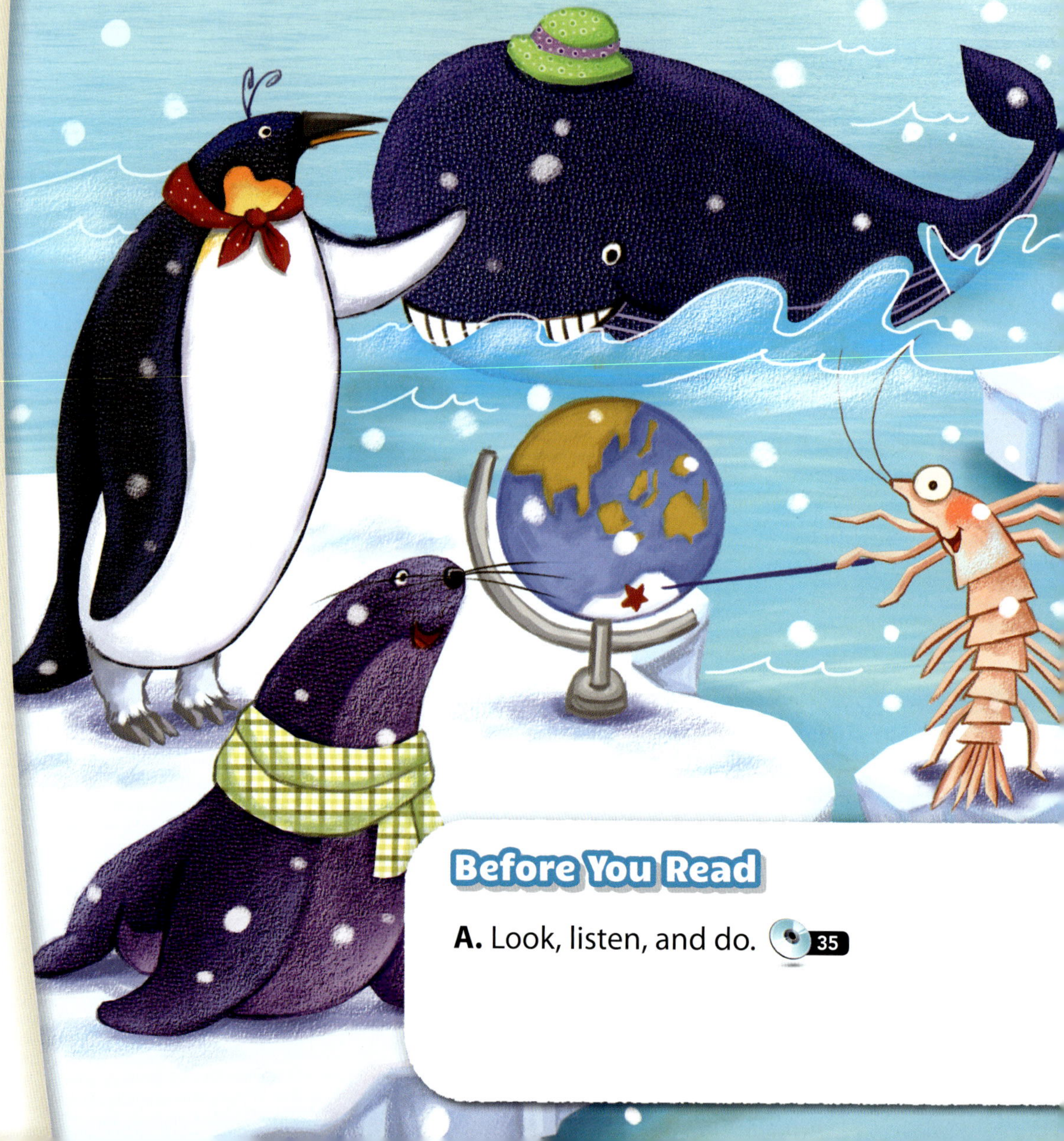

Before You Read

A. Look, listen, and do.  35

We have a lot of snow and ice.
We have a lot of strong winds.
We have some volcanoes.

However, we don't have rain.

Rain quickly becomes snow or ice.

Come and try ice walks and sledding with us!

these   live   come   try

Read for Oral Reading Fluency

A. Listen to the story.  36

B. Read together.

C. Read together again.  37

Stand up and sit down when you read the word "we." 

Retell

A **Focus Skill** **Where does Penguin live? Choose and say.**

I live in the (Arctic / Antarctic).

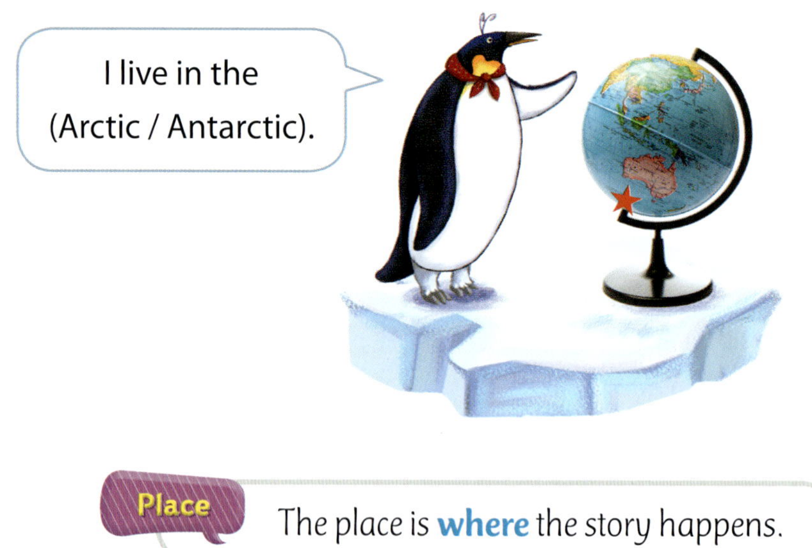

Place The place is **where** the story happens.

B **Retell** **Write and retell about the Antarctic.**

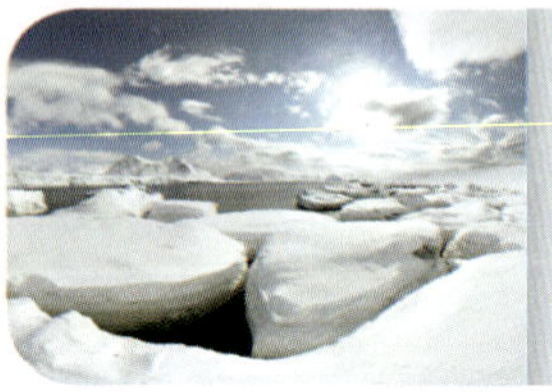

We have a lot of snow and ....

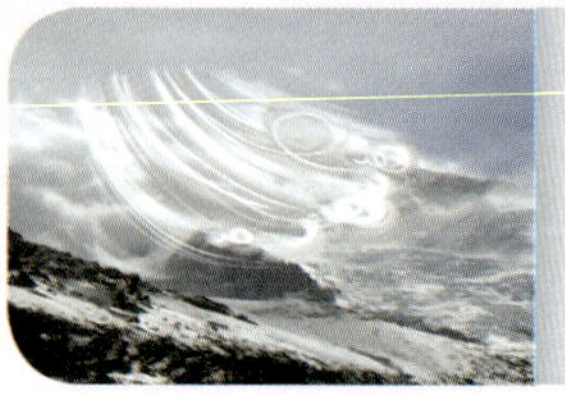

We have a lot of strong ....

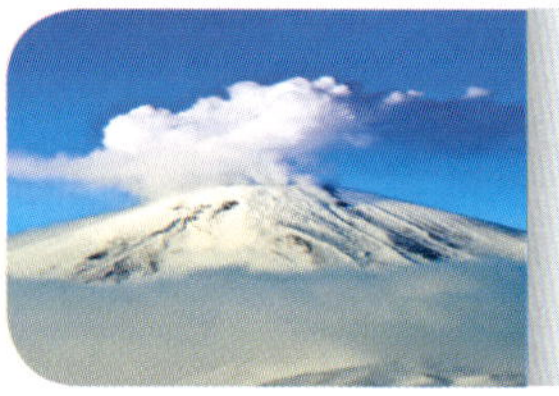

We have some ....

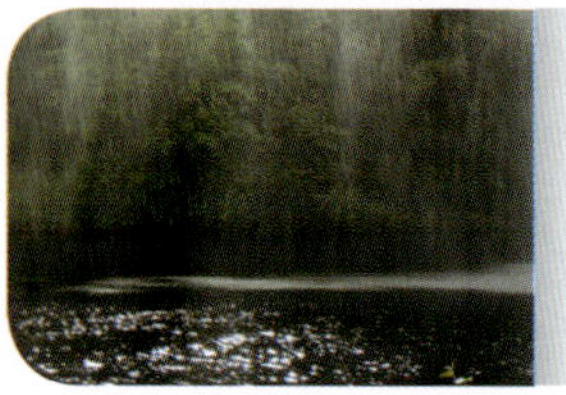

We don't have ....

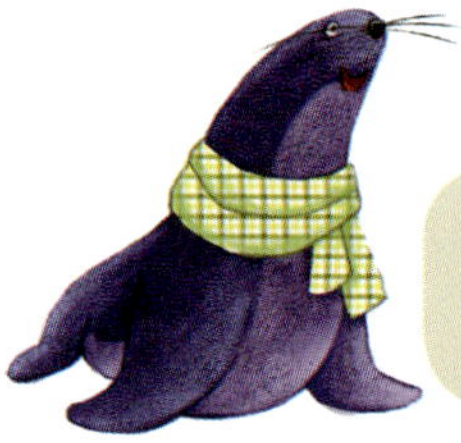

ice	rain
volcanoes	winds

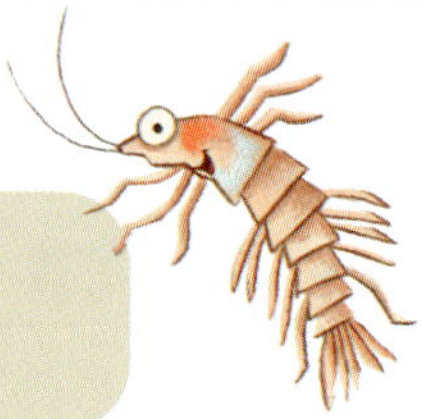

Comprehension

1. **What is the story about?**

   a. the Antarctic   **b.** the weather   **c.** the friends

2. **What becomes snow in the Antarctic?**

   a. ice   **b.** rain   **c.** wind

3. **They have a lot of strong ____________.**

   a. clouds   **b.** winds   **c.** volcanoes

4. **In the Antarctic, they don't have ____________.**

   a.    **b.**    **c.** 

Literacy Center Pronunciation

- **Listen and repeat.**  38

  th: sou**th**   mou**th**   tee**th**

  th: **th**ese   **th**at   bro**th**er

  There are **th**ree tee**th** in the mou**th**.

A Lion and a Skunk `Fiction`

follow

grass

woods

hole

roar

fart

Tiptoe! Tiptoe! Tiptoe! Tiptoe!
A hungry lion follows after a skunk.
The skunk goes through tall grass.
The skunk goes through the woods.

Before You Read

A. Look, listen, and do. 

The skunk goes into a hole.
The lion follows the skunk
into the hole.
Grrrrr! The lion roars loudly.
The skunk is surprised.

Boom!
The skunk farts!
"Yikes! What a bad smell!"
The lion runs away.

goes   through   into   away

Read for Oral Reading Fluency

A. Listen to the story. 

B. Read together.

C. Read together again. 

Read "Tiptoe" softly, and "Grrrrr," "Boom," and "Yikes" loudly.

Retell

A **Focus Skill** Where does this story happen? Choose three places.

Place The place is **where** the story happens.

B **Retell** Read and number in order. Retell the story to your partner.

A hungry lion follows after a skunk.

The skunk farts and the lion runs away.

The lion follows the skunk into the hole.

Tip! First → Next → Then

46

Comprehension

1. **What is the story about?**

   a. a lion and a skunk   **b.** the woods   **c.** farting

2. **The lion follows the skunk through tall _____________.**

   a. trees   **b.** holes   **c.** grass

3. **The lion runs away because of the bad _____________.**

   a. noise   **b.** smell   **c.** taste

4. **How does the skunk feel when the lion roars loudly?**

   a.    **b.**    **c.** 

Literacy Center Grammar

- **Listen and repeat.**  43

What a bad smell!	What a good idea!
What a smart skunk!	What a stupid lion!

Dinosaurs 

Words  

dinosaur

claw

frill

horn

plate

spike

Dinosaurs lived a long time ago.
Look at the pictures.
They are all different.

Baryonyx has very long claws.
They are on its hands.

Before You Read

A. Look, listen, and do. 45

48

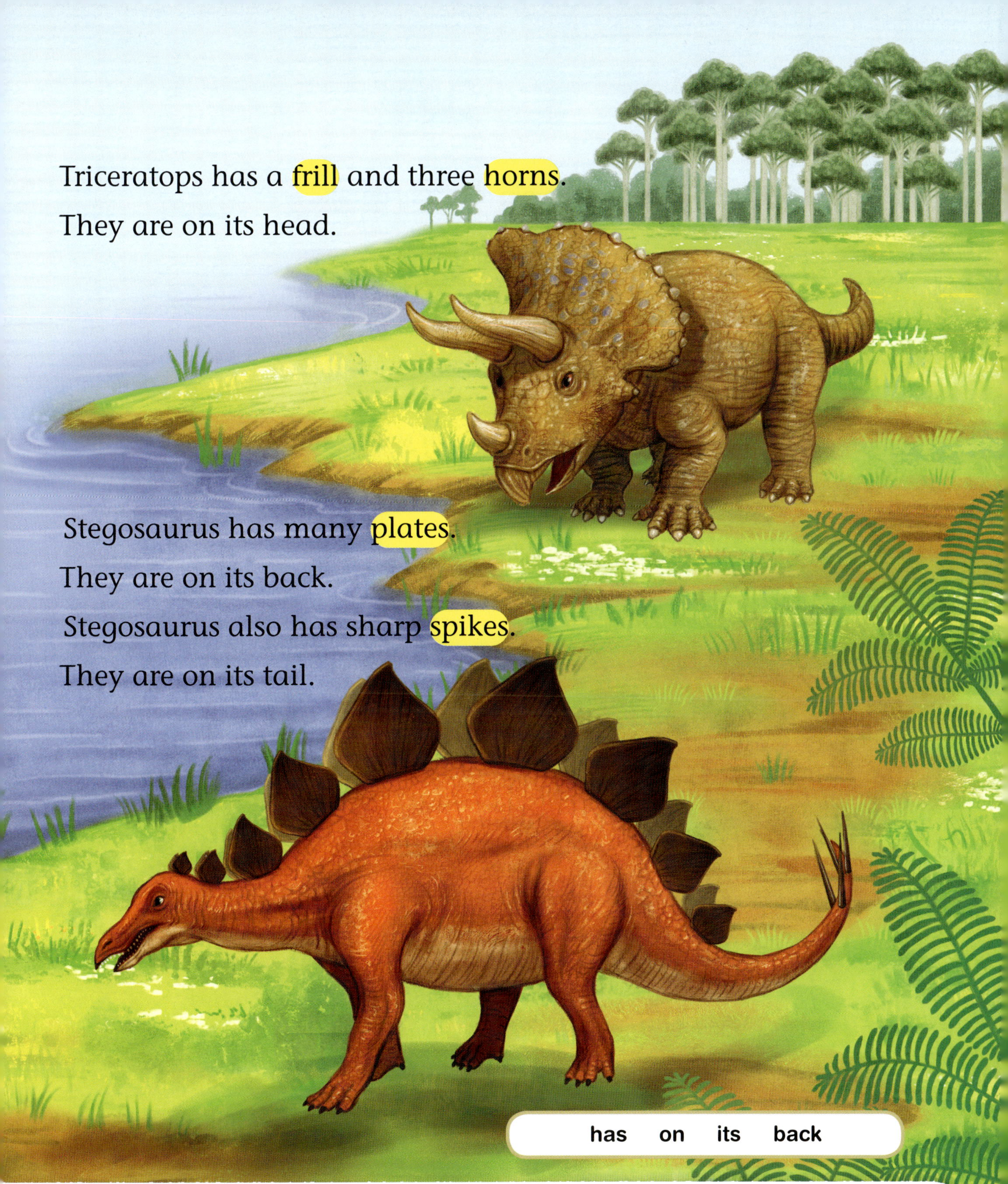

Triceratops has a frill and three horns.
They are on its head.

Stegosaurus has many plates.
They are on its back.
Stegosaurus also has sharp spikes.
They are on its tail.

has on its back

Read for Oral Reading Fluency

A. Listen to the story. 46

B. Read together.

C. Read together again. 47

They *are on its* (**hands**).

A **Focus Skill** Read what the main idea and details are.

> **Main Idea & Details** The main idea is the **big idea** in the story.
> Details **tell more** about the main idea.

B **Retell** Draw the missing body parts of the three dinosaurs.
Then, retell about them.

Main idea Dinosaurs are all different.

Detail 1: Baryonyx

It has very long claws
on its hands.

Detail 2: Triceratops

It has a frill and three horns
on its head.

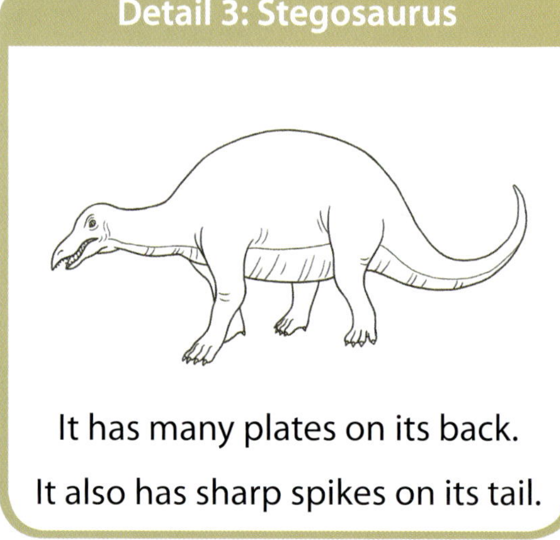

Detail 3: Stegosaurus

It has many plates on its back.

It also has sharp spikes on its tail.

Comprehension

1. **What is the story about?**

   a. Dinosaurs lived a long time ago.

   b. Dinosaurs look the same.

   c. Dinosaurs look different.

2. **Baryonyx's claws are very ____________.**

   a. thin   **b.** short   **c.** long

3. **Which dinosaur has a frill?**

   a. Triceratops   **b.** Stegosaurus   **c.** Baryonyx

4. **Stegosaurus doesn't have ____________.**

   a.    **b.**    **c.** 

Literacy Center High Frequency Words

- **Read "Dinosaurs" again. Find and mark ○, △, and □.**

  has = ○   on = △   its = □

- **How many ○, △, and □ did you find? Compare with your partner.**

Retell

A  Focus Skill Read what the plot is.

Plot A story's plot is **what happens** in the beginning, middle, and end of the story.

B Retell Match and retell about Allen and his dad.

| Beginning | Middle | End |

Dad's phone rings and he answers it.

Allen gets his first cell phone.

Allen plays a game at the dinner table.

Comprehension

1. **What is the story about?**

   a. car manners

   b. table manners

   c. playground manners

2. **Allen downloads some** ____________.

   a. songs **b.** games **c.** computers

3. **When does the story happen?**

   a. at breakfast **b.** at lunch **c.** at dinner

4. **Who answers the phone at the table?**

   a.  **b.**  **c.** 

Literacy Center Pronunciation

- **Listen and repeat.**  52

er: dinner	manner	He has good dinner manners.
ir: first	bird	The first girl has a bird.
ur: turn	burger	Turn the card and see the burger.

Unit 13

Don't Tease the Monkeys

Fiction

Words

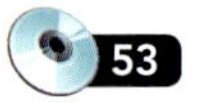

53

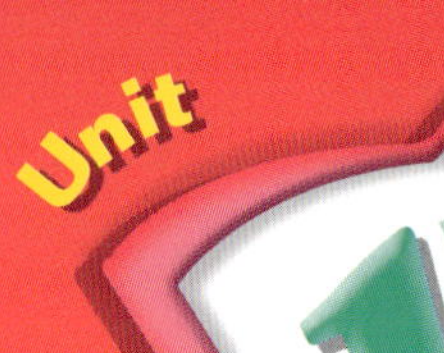

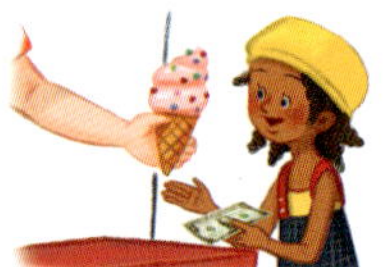

buy

ice cream

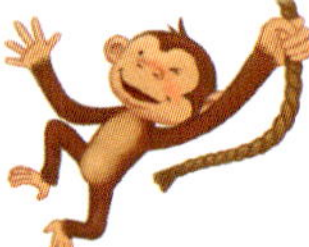

monkey

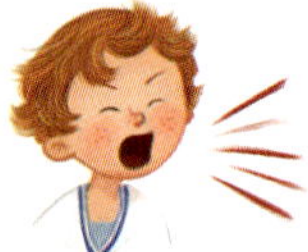

yell

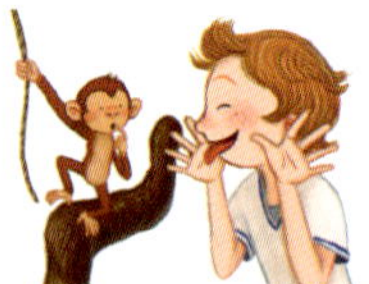

tease

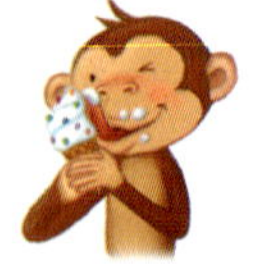

eat

Ken and Alice buy ice cream.

They go to see the monkeys at the zoo.

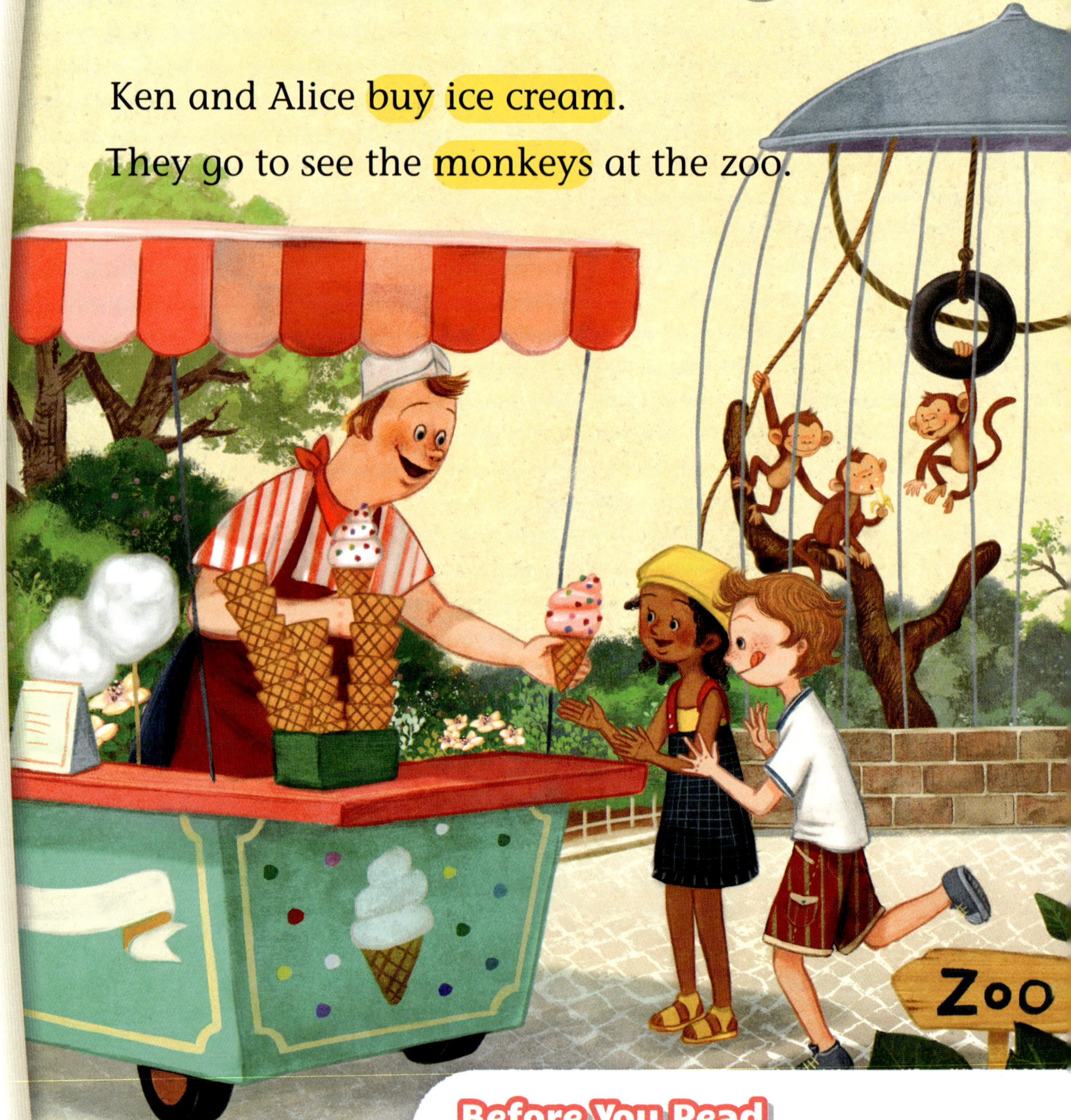

Before You Read

A. Look, listen, and do. 54

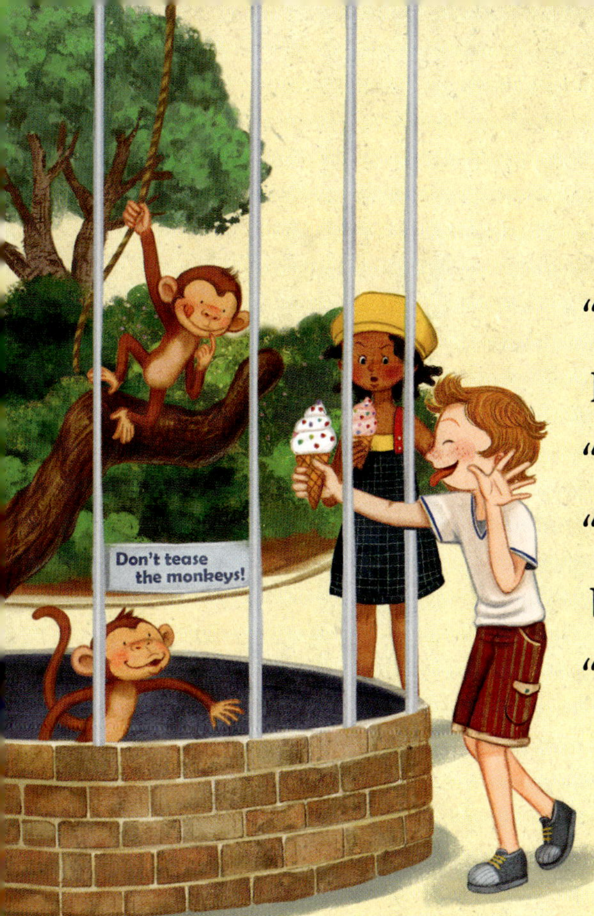

"Hey, monkeys! Here is ice cream."
Ken yells and teases the monkeys.
"Don't tease the monkeys," says Alice.
"They might take your ice cream."
But, Ken doesn't listen.
"Hey, monkeys! Here is ice cream."

Suddenly, a monkey runs toward Ken.
It takes his ice cream and eats it.

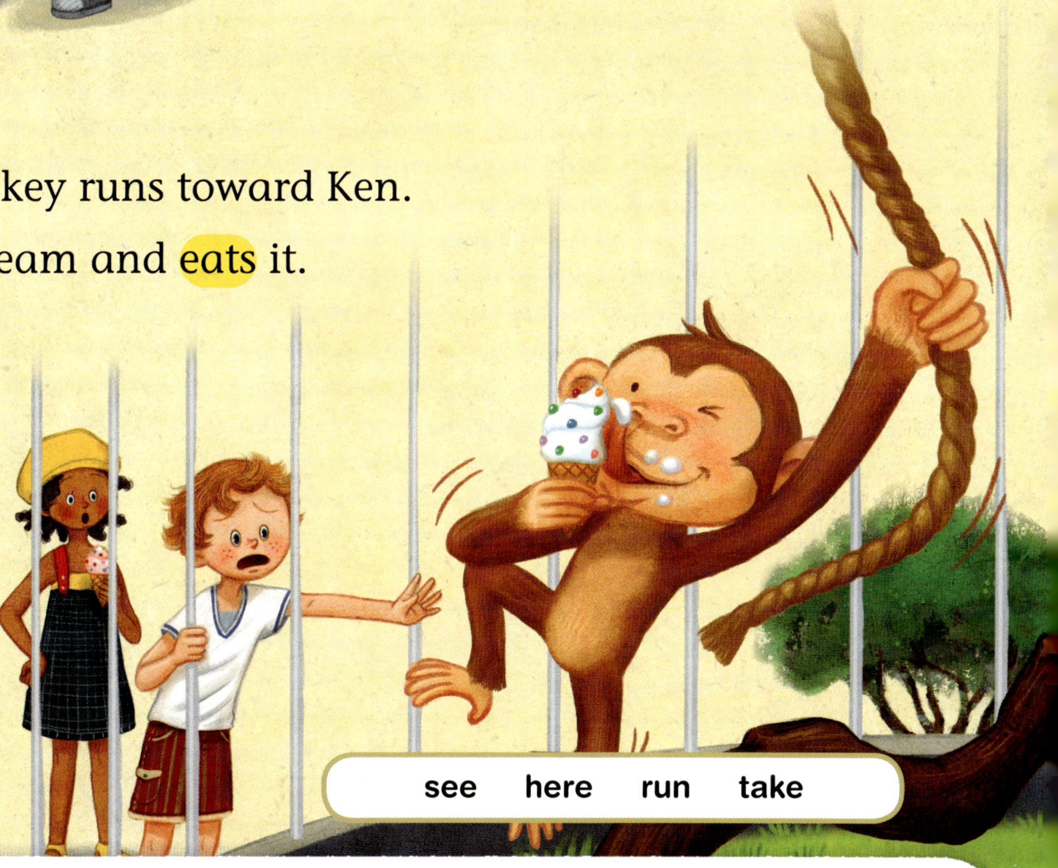

see **here** **run** **take**

Read for Oral Reading Fluency

A. Listen to the story. 55

B. Read together.

C. Read together again. 56

Clap and stamp when you read the story.

ice cream = (clap) monkey = (stamp)

A **Focus Skill** **What happens at the end of the story?**

Plot A story's plot is **what happens** in the beginning, middle, and end of the story.

B **Retell** **Read and number in order. Retell the story to your partner.**

A monkey takes Ken's ice cream and eats it.

Ken and Alice buy ice cream. They go to see the monkeys at the zoo.

Ken yells and teases the monkeys with his ice cream.

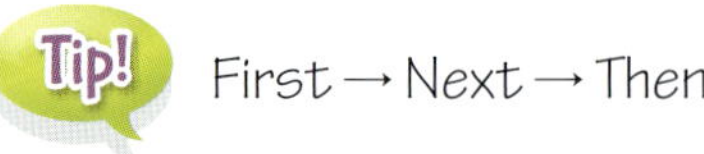

Tip! First → Next → Then

Comprehension

1. **What is the story about?**

   a. buying ice cream

   b. teasing monkeys

   c. playing with monkeys

2. **Where are Ken and Alice?**

   a. at the zoo   **b.** at the store   **c.** at the circus

3. **Ken teases the monkeys with his ___________.**

   a.    **b.**    **c.** 

4. **___________ takes Ken's ice cream and eats it.**

   a. A monkey   **b.** Ken   **c.** Alice

- **Listen and repeat.**  57

  Tease the monkeys.   Don't tease the monkeys.

  Buy ice cream.   Don't buy ice cream.

A **Focus Skill**   Read what the main idea and details are.

Main Idea & Details   The main idea is the **big idea** in the story.
Details **tell more** about the main idea.

B **Retell**   Write and retell about the polite words.

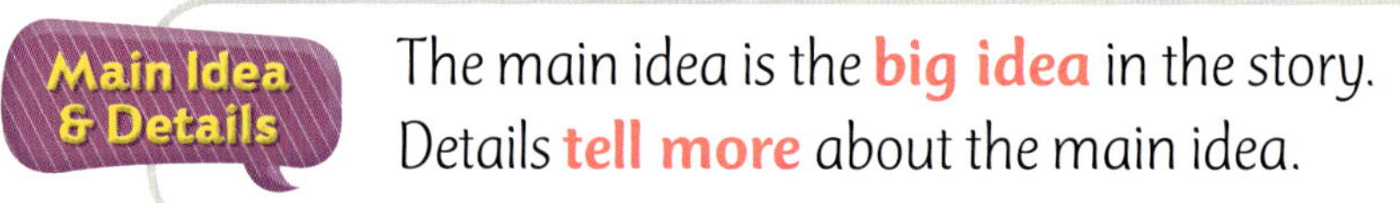

Comprehension

1. **What is the story about?**

   a. using polite words

   b. saying hello

   c. remembering polite words

2. **Polite words make people feel ___________ .**

   a. bad   **b.** happy   **c.** sorry

3. **Say "___________" when you want something.**

   a. Please   **b.** Thank you   **c.** You're welcome

4. **When do you say "Excuse me"?**

   a.    **b.**    **c.** 

Literacy Center High Frequency Words

- **Listen and circle the same words. Then count them.**  62

1. **you**	you	your	you	you	( )
2. **when**	when	where	what	who	( )
3. **say**	say	day	say	sat	( )

Read & Retell 2

Bird-Watching

Unit 15 — Reading Day

We will read a story about Ira, Ed, and Grandpa.
Ira, Ed, and Grandpa go to the bird park.

Unit 16 — Retelling Day

We will retell the story, "Bird-Watching."

Words

Listen and repeat.  63

bird

park

woodpecker

peck

hammer

kookaburra

Before You Read

Picture A   Where are they?

Picture B   What is the bird doing?

15

Bird-Watching

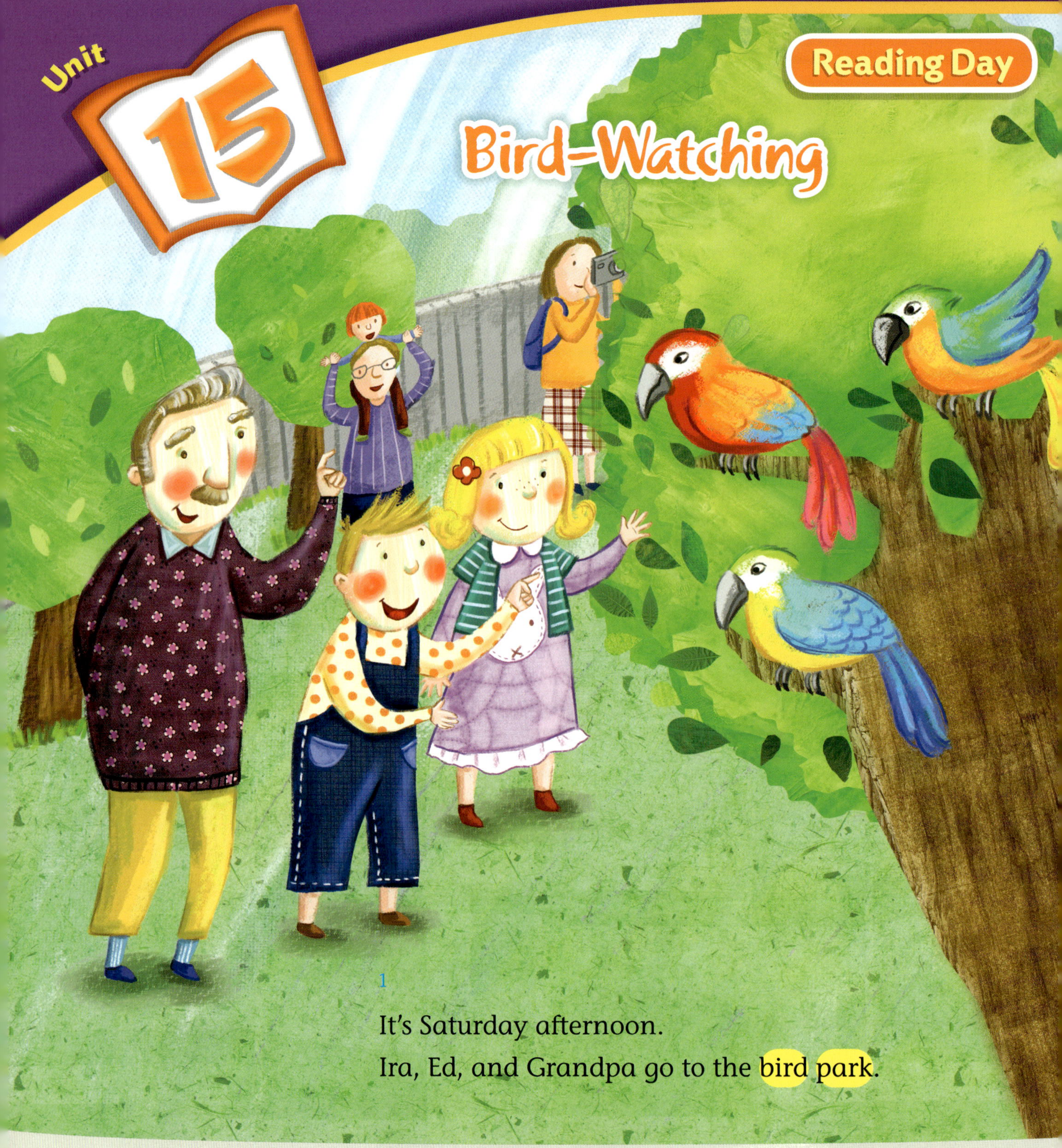

1

It's Saturday afternoon.
Ira, Ed, and Grandpa go to the bird park.

Read for Oral Reading Fluency

A. Listen to the story. 

B. Read together.

C. Read together again. 

Use different voices for each character.

 Do you see that bird?

 It's a woodpecker.

Toc, toc, toc! It pecks.
It sounds like hammering!

3

 Do you see that bird?

 It's a kookaburra.

 Koo koo kakakaka! It sings.
It sounds like laughing!

4

 Bird-watching is fun!

Let's come here again next week.

do   that   sound   like

✓ **Quick Check-Up**

	True	False
1. Ira and Ed are in the woods.	☐	☐
2. A kookaburra makes a hammering sound.	☐	☐
3. Ira likes bird-watching.	☐	☐

Comprehension

A. Read and circle the correct answers.

Ira, Ed, and Grandpa go to the (bird / bear) park.

A woodpecker (sings / pecks).

It sounds like (hammering / laughing)!

A (woodpecker / kookaburra) sings.

It (looks / sounds) like laughing!

B. Read the story again. Then, guess what will happen after the story.

Ed will say, "________________________."

Ira, Ed, and Grandpa go to
the bird park.

Grandpa says, "Let's come
here again next week."

They see a kookaburra.
Koo koo kakakaka! It sounds
like laughing!

They see a woodpecker.
Toc, toc, toc! It sounds like
hammering!

Bird-Watching

Retelling Day Routine

A Read the story.

D Retell the story.

B Arrange the retelling cards.

E Write a summary.

C Make a retelling chart.

A Read — Read the story on pages 66 and 67.

B Arrange

1. Cut out the retelling cards, and write the numbers in order.
2. Check the order with your teacher.

Retelling Chart 2

C **Make**

1. Complete the **red** speech bubbles. (Hints are at the back of the cards.)
2. **Glue** the retelling cards.
3. Complete the **blue** speech bubbles.

name

BIRD PARK

D **Retell**   Retell the story with your retelling chart.

How to Retell

1. Hold up your retelling chart.
2. Retell the story using the speech bubbles.
3. Use **First**, **Next**, **Then**, and **Last**.

Tips!
- Stand tall.
- Speak clearly.
- Make eye contact.

E **Write**   1. Write a summary using your retelling chart.

2. After you finish, listen to Justin's retelling.  66

First, Ira, Ed, and Grandpa go ______________________________.

Next, they see ______________________. Toc, toc, toc!

It ______________________!

Then, they see ______________________. Koo koo kakakaka!

______________________!

Last, Grandpa says, " ______________________."

[1~4] Choose the correct answers.

1. 
   a. soccer
   b. glasses
   c. basketball

2.
   a. art
   b. gym
   c. balloon

3. 
   a. dribble
   b. fold
   c. frown

4.
   a. thick
   b. scribble
   c. bounce

[5~7] Choose the correct answers.

5. My grandfather wears thick _____________.

   a. chair
   b. balloon
   c. glasses

6. My sister bounces the _____________.

   a. ball
   b. book
   c. desk

7. I _____________ a picture in the art room.

   a. play
   b. draw
   c. frown

[8~9] Read the story and circle True or False.

Bill, Sam, and Tina are at the playground.
"What shall we play?" says Bill.
"Let's play soccer," says Sam.
He dribbles the ball.

8. Bill doesn't want to play with Sam and Tina.　　True　　False

9. Sam wants to play soccer.　　True　　False

[10~11] Read the story and choose the correct answers.

Where are the students?
They are in the art room.
They draw pictures in the art room.

Where are they?
They are in the gym.
They play basketball in the gym.

10. Which place is not in the story?

   a. an art room　　　b. a library　　　c. a gym

11. Students play ______________ in the gym.

   a. music　　　b. computer games　　c. basketball

[1~4] Choose the correct answers.

1. 

   a. worried
   b. nervous
   c. proud

2. 

   a. rock
   b. puddle
   c. stair

3. 

   a. vegetable
   b. fast food
   c. soda

4. 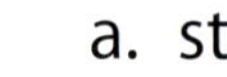

   a. stand
   b. cheer
   c. hurry

[5~7] Choose the correct answers.

5. Tommy _____________ a song in music class.

   a. stands　　　　b. jumps　　　　c. performs

6. The _____________ is really hard.

   a. soda　　　　b. rock　　　　c. puddle

7. Carrots and beans are _____________.

   a. vegetables　　　　b. sweets　　　　c. fast food

[8~9] Read the story and circle True or False.

Today is Friday.
Judy performs a song in music class.
She stands tall and sings loudly.
Everyone claps and cheers.

8. Judy sings a song in music class.   True   False

9. Judy's friends don't like her song.   True   False

[10~11] Read the story and choose the correct answers.

There are many snacks around us.
Fruits and vegetables are good for us.
Fast food, sweets, and soda are bad for us.

10. _______________ are good snacks.

    a. Sweets   b. Fruits   c. Hamburgers

11. Which snack is bad for us?

    a. a banana   b. an orange   c. a chocolate bar

[1~4] Choose the correct answers.

1. 
   a. wind
   b. grass
   c. volcano

2. 
   a. plate
   b. woods
   c. hole

3. 
   a. claw
   b. horn
   c. spike

4. 
   a. sled
   b. follow
   c. roar

[5~7] Choose the correct answers.

5. The dinosaur has a long ____________.

   a. smell   b. horn   c. wind

6. I ____________ the dog into the park.

   a. go   b. roar   c. follow

7. There is a lot of ____________ in the Antarctic.

   a. grass   b. ice   c. dinosaurs

[8~9] Read the story and circle True or False.

Hi! I'm Penguin.

Whale, Seal, Krill, and I live in the Antarctic.

We have a lot of snow and ice.

We have some volcanoes.

However, we don't have rain.

8. Penguin lives in a cold place.   True   False

9. There are no volcanoes in the Antarctic.   True   False

[10~11] Read the story and choose the correct answers.

Dinosaurs are all different.

Baryonyx has very long claws.

They are on its hands.

Triceratops has a frill and three horns.

They are on its head.

Stegosaurus has sharp spikes.

They are on its tail.

10.   What does Baryonyx have?

   a. a frill   b. claws   c. horns

11.   Stegosaurus has spikes on its ____________.

   a. tail   b. head   c. hands

[1~4] Choose the correct answers.

1. 
   a. dinner
   b. game
   c. ice cream

2.
   a. buy
   b. eat
   c. thank

3. 
   a. burp
   b. yell
   c. sneeze

4. 
   a. want
   b. tease
   c. answer

[5~7] Choose the correct answers.

5. Don't ____________ on the school bus.

   a. yell   b. want   c. mistake

6. My cell phone ____________ loudly.

   a. rings   b. minds   c. downloads

7. When your friend ____________ you, say "You're welcome."

   a. burps   b. thanks   c. makes

[8~9] Read the story and circle True or False.

> Allen gets his first cell phone.
> He plays a game at the dinner table.
> "Mind your manners, Allen. Play after dinner," says Dad.

8. Allen plays a game at dinner.　　　　　True　　False

9. Allen has good table manners.　　　　　True　　False

[10~11] Read the story and choose the correct answers.

> There are some polite words.
> When you want something, say "Please."
> When you make a mistake, say "I am sorry."
> When you burp or sneeze, say "Excuse me."
> Then people will be happy.

10. Say "＿＿＿＿＿＿" when you make a mistake.

　　a. Please　　　　　b. Excuse me　　　　　c. I am sorry

11. What words make people happy?

　　a. easy words　　　　b. polite words　　　　c. bad words

Supplementary Materials

- **Word List**
- **Read & Retell Sheets**
- **Retelling Cards**

Word List

Unit 1

thick
glasses
library
frown
fold
scribble

Unit 2

playground
soccer
dribble
ball
balloon
bounce

Unit 3

art
draw
picture
cafeteria
gym
basketball

Unit 4

perform
worried
nervous
stand
cheer
proud

Unit 5

April
hurry
puddle
rock
stair
messy

Unit 6

vegetable
full
healthy
fast food
soda
unhealthy

Unit 7

trick
scream
chair
spider
hate
laugh

Word List

Unit 9

krill
Antarctic
ice
wind
volcano
sled

Unit 10

follow
grass
woods
hole
roar
fart

Unit 11

dinosaur
claw
frill
horn
plate
spike

Unit 12

cell phone
download
game
dinner
ring
answer

Unit 13

buy
ice cream
monkey
yell
tease
eat

Unit 14

polite
want
thank
mistake
burp
sneeze

Unit 15

bird
park
woodpecker
peck
hammer
kookaburra

Read & Retell Sheet – Fiction

Make a copy and use this when you **read and retell** a fiction story.

Title: _______________________________

Characters	
Place	
Time	
Plot	**Beginning**
	Middle
	End

Unit 1   Unit 1   Unit 1

Unit 2   Unit 2   Unit 2

Unit 3   Unit 3   Unit 3

Retelling Cards Unit 4~Unit 6

Retell the story using the retelling cards.

Unit 4

Unit 4

Unit 4

Unit 5

Unit 5

Unit 5

Unit 6

Unit 6

Unit 6

Retelling Cards Unit 9~Unit 11

Retell the story using the retelling cards.

Unit 9

Unit 9

Unit 9

Unit 10

Unit 10

Unit 10

Unit 11

Unit 11

Unit 11

Retelling Cards

Retell the story using the retelling cards.

Unit 12

Unit 12

Unit 12

Unit 13

Unit 13

Unit 13

Unit 14

Unit 14

Unit 14

LEVEL GUIDE NE_Build & Grow Products

Category	Level			Primary							Secondary		Components
	Books	Lexile®	Kindergarten	Low Beginner	Beginner	High Beginner	Low Intermediate	Intermediate	High Intermediate	A	B	
Phonics	Phonics Show 1,2,3,4		●	●									Student Book/ Workbook/ 2 MultiROMs
	Phonics Show Readers 1,2,3,4		●	●									Book/ Audio CD
	Come On, Phonics 1, 2, 3, 4, 5		●	●									Student Book/ Workbook/ Readers/ DVD-ROM
Readers	Show Time L1,2,3			●	●	●							Student Book/ Workbook/ MultiROM
Coursebook	Come On, Everyone 1,2,3,4,5,6			●	●	●							Student Book/ Workbook/ Teacher's Book / DVD-ROM
Reading	Reading Sketch Starter 1,2,3	BR	●	●									Student Book/ Workbook/ MultiROM
	Reading Sketch 1,2,3	170L~210L		●	●								Student Book/ Workbook/ Audio CD
	Reading Sketch Up 1,2,3	260L~300L			●	●							Student Book/ Workbook/ Audio CD
	Reading Sponge 1,2,3	160L~280L		●	●								Student Book/ Workbook/ MultiROM
	Read & Retell 1,2,3	240L~390L			●	●							Student Book/ Workbook/ Audio CD
	Reading Sense 1,2,3	320L~410L				●							Student Book/ Workbook/ Audio CD
	Reading Clue 1,2,3	490L~510L					●						Student Book/ Workbook/ Audio CD
	The Basic Way 1,2,3 (2nd Edition)	570L~660L					●	●					Student Book/ Workbook/ MultiROM
	Read to Reach 1,2,3	600L~660L						●					Student Book/ Workbook/ Audio CD
	The Best Way 1,2,3 (2nd Edition)	860L~970L								●	●		Student Book/ Workbook/ MultiROM
	Reading Source 1,2,3	580L~710L						●	●				Student Book/ Workbook/ Audio CD
	Reading Peak 1,2,3	860L~900L								●	●		Student Book/ Workbook/ Audio CD
	Read Up 1,2,3	1070L~1320L										●	Student Book/ Supplementary Material/ MP3 CD
	Easy Link Starter 1,2,3		●	●									Student Book/ Workbook/ MultiROM
	Easy Link 1,2,3	240L~280L		●									Student Book/ Workbook/ MultiROM

Workbook
Retell
Oral Reading Fluency
Literacy Center

Retelling Cards Included

Read & Retell
1   
NE_Build & Grow

Read & Retell 1

Workbook

NE_Build & Grow

1 Mr. Frown the Librarian

name:

score:

Words

A. Choose the correct letters and rewrite the words.

1.

(c / g)lasses

2.

libr(a / e)ry

3.

fo(r / l)d

4.

thi(k / ck)

5.

scri(bb / dd)le

6.

frow(n / m)

Literacy Center Pronunciation

B. Read and circle the words with the same sounds.

1. **fr**own   **fr**og   **fl**ower   **fr**iend

2. **gl**asses   **gr**ow   **gl**ove   **gl**ue

3. **sm**ile   **sm**art   **sn**ow   **sm**all

Comprehension

C. Read the story on pages 8 and 9. Then match the sentence parts.

1.	Mr. Frown is	quietly.
2.	Mr. Frown	the page.
3.	Ann scribbles on	wears thick glasses.
4.	Ann reads a book	tall and thin.

Summary with the Retelling Cards

D. Number in order. Then rewrite the summary below.

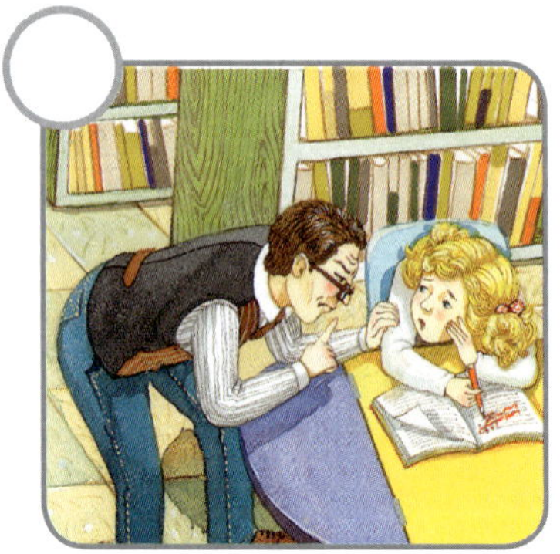

Ann folds the page.
Mr. Frown frowns.

1

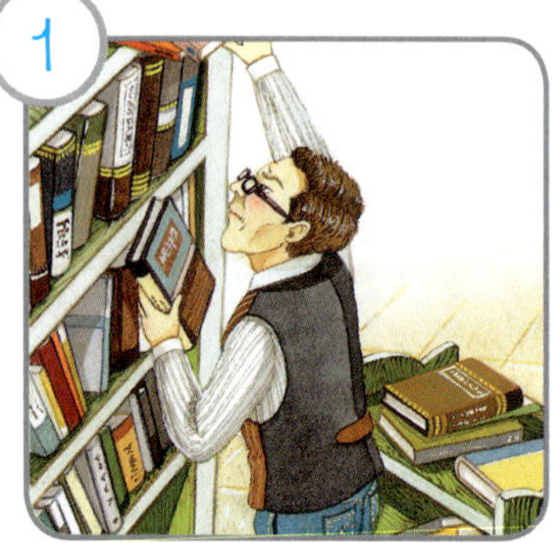

Mr. Frown works at the school library.

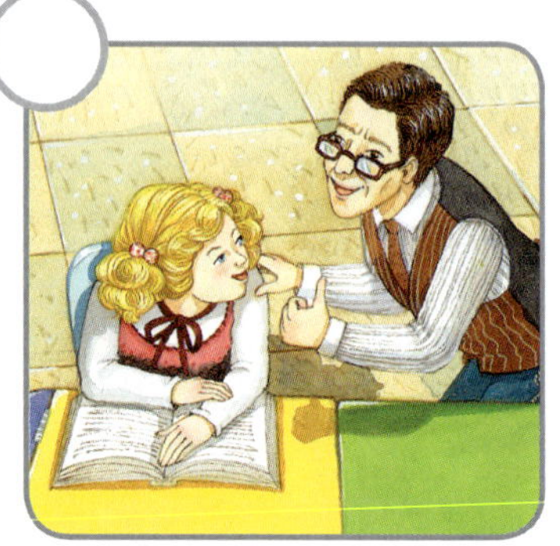

Ann reads a book quietly.
Mr. Frown smiles.

1 **Beginning** Mr. Frown works at the school library.

2 **Middle**

3 **End**

Let's Play!

name:

score:

A. Circle the correct words and match them with the pictures.

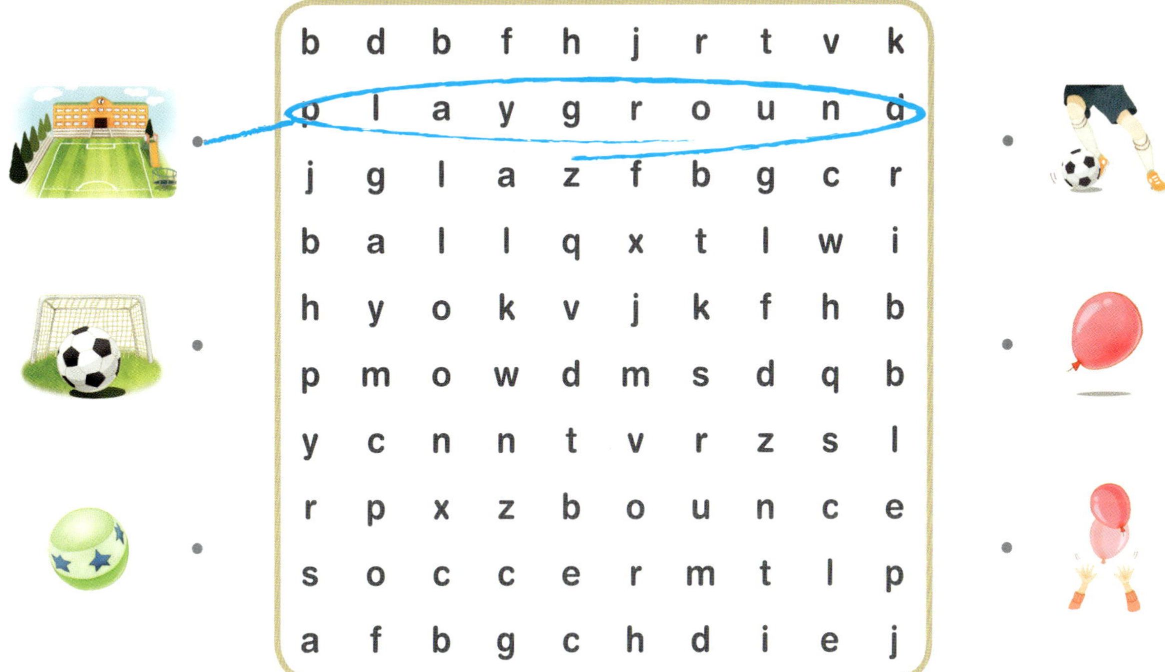

B. Circle the correct words and read the sentences.

1. Let's (play / plays) soccer.

2. Let's (dribbled / dribble) the ball.

3. Let's (bouncing / bounce) the ball.

C. **Read the story on pages 12 and 13. Then circle True or False.**

1. Tina bounces the balloon.   True   False

2. Bill wants to play soccer.   True   False

Summary with the Retelling Cards

D. **Circle the correct words. Then rewrite the summary below.**

1. Sam wants to play (soccer / basketball).

2. He (throws / dribbles) the ball.

3. Tina wants to play with a (ball / balloon).

4. She (bounces / kicks) it.

5. They play (soccer / balloon soccer) together.

Places at School

name:

score:

Words

A. Fill in the missing letters and rewrite the words.

1. 

a [ ] t

____

2. 

gy [ ]

____

3. 

p [ ] ct [ ] re

____

4. 

[ ] asketb [ ] ll

____

5. 

d [ ] a [ ]

____

6. 

ca [ ] ete [ ] ia

____

Literacy Center High Frequency Words

B. Write the correct words and read the sentences.

| are | they | the |

1. _______________ are in the cafeteria.

2. Where are _______________ students?

3. There _______________ many places at school.

C. Read the story on pages 16 and 17. Then circle True or False.

1. Students have a delicious lunch in the art room.   True   False

2. Students play basketball in the gym.   True   False

Summary with the Retelling Cards

D. Write the correct words. Then rewrite the summary below.

There are many ___________ at school. Students draw pictures in the ___________. They have a delicious lunch in the ___________. They play basketball in the ___________.

art room   cafeteria   places   gym

Friday Music Class

name:

score:

Words

A. Unscramble the letters to make the words.

1. 

ou / pr / d

----

2. 

ed / ri / wor

----

3. 

nd / a / st

----

4. 

s / vou / ner

----

5. 

e / ch / er

----

6. 

per / m / for

Literacy Center Pronunciation

B. Read and circle the words with the different sounds.

1. _a_pple   cat   ham   cake

2. r_a_t   class   p_a_ge   after

3. st_a_nd   t_a_pe   clap   after

C. Read the story on pages 20 and 21. Then match the sentence parts.

1. Today	worried.
2. I have to	and cheers.
3. I feel	perform a song.
4. Everyone claps	is Friday.

Summary with the Retelling Cards

D. Number in order. Then rewrite the summary below.

It's music class. I stand tall and sing loudly. I feel proud.

My music class is after lunch. I feel nervous.

It's art class. I have to perform a song in music class.

1	Beginning	....
2	Middle	....
3	End	....

Henry Hurry Hurries

name:

score:

Words

A. Complete the crossword puzzle.

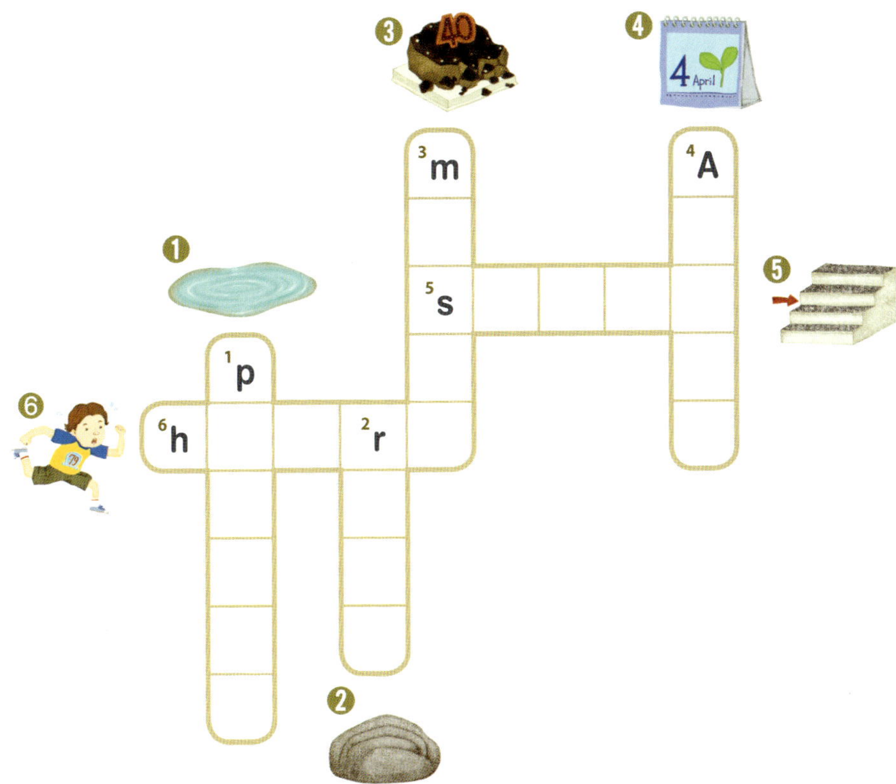

Literacy Center Grammar

B. Write the correct forms of the words.

1. four – fourth   five – (   )

2. six – (   )   seven – seventh

3. eight – eighth   nine – (   )

C. **Read the story on pages 24 and 25. Then circle True or False.**

1. Henry jumps down the stairs.　　　　　　True　　False

2. Henry jumps over the rock.　　　　　　True　　False

D. **Circle the correct words. Then rewrite the summary below.**

1. Henry buys a (chocolate / cheese) cake for his mother.

2. It is his mother's (fourth / fortieth) birthday.

3. Henry hurries to his (school / house).

4. He jumps up the (puddle / stairs).

5. The cake is messy. But his mother says, "It's still (salty / sweet)."

12

Good Snacks and Bad Snacks

name:

score:

Words

A. Fill in the missing letters and rewrite the words.

1.

f ☐ l ☐

2.

h ☐ al ☐ hy

3.

☐ o ☐ a

B. Circle the related words.

1. **vegetable**   banana   carrot   orange

2. **fast food**   hamburger   grape   cucumber

3. **unhealthy**   vitamin   mineral   sugar

Literacy Center High Frequency Words

C. Write the correct words and read the sentences.

and   for   full

1. Some snacks are bad _________ us.

2. They are _________ of sugar and salt.

3. Fruits _________ vegetables are good for us.

D.   **Read the story on pages 28 and 29. Then circle True or False.**

1. Sweets are good for us.   True   False

2. Fruits are full of vitamins and minerals.   True   False

Summary with the Retelling Cards

E.   **Write the correct words. Then rewrite the summary below.**

Some snacks are good, and some snacks are bad. Fruits and ________________ are good for us. They make us ________________. Fast food, sweets, and ________________ are bad for us. They make us ________________.

healthy	soda	unhealthy	vegetables

April Fools' Day!

name:

score:

Words

A. Choose the correct letters and rewrite the words.

1. 

(s / c)hair

2. 

s(f / p)ider

3. 

(t / d)rick

4. 

scre(a / e)m

5. 

lau(g / p)h

6. 

h(a / i)te

B. Circle the related words.

1. **spider**	food	plant	animal
2. **laugh**	sad	happy	angry
3. **chair**	sit	stand	lie

C.   **Read the story on pages 34 and 35. Then choose the best answers.**

   1. What is the story about?

      a. a spider   **b.** Robin's chair   **c.** April Fools' Day

   2. Robin and Emma are in the ___________.

      a. classroom   **b.** playground   **c.** art room

   3. Who runs to the front of the classroom?

      a. Emma   **b.** Robin   **c.** Robin's teacher

   4. What does Robin hate?

      a.   **b.**   **c.**

   5. The story happens in ___________.

      a. March   **b.** April   **c.** May

April Fools' Day!

name:

score:

Words

A. Circle the correct words and match them with the pictures.

i	l	m	b	t	s	f	v	s	k
h	a	t	e	l	y	g	k	d	y
m	u	c	d	d	v	s	t	r	a
s	g	s	f	t	f	p	s	j	n
c	h	a	i	r	c	i	j	b	g
j	z	w	g	z	q	d	f	c	h
u	k	y	s	c	r	e	a	m	w
l	g	o	l	k	e	r	d	o	n
a	t	r	i	c	k	x	b	l	c
d	q	c	a	r	r	a	z	t	f

B. Circle the related words.

1. hate   frown   smile   laugh

2. scream   proud   sad   scared

C. Number in order. Then rewrite the summary below.

(   ) Next, Emma says, "Robin! There is a spider under your chair!"

(   ) First, Emma goes to school early. She wants to trick Robin.

(   ) He asks, "Where is the spider?"

(   ) Last, Emma laughs and says, "April Fools!"

(   ) Then, Robin screams and jumps out of his chair.

We Live in the Antarctic

name:

score:

Words

A. Choose the correct letters and rewrite the words.

1.
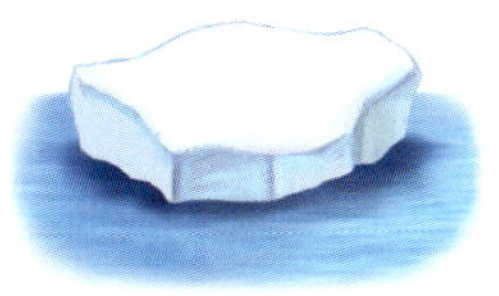
i(s / c)e

2.

(k / c)rill

3.

An(d / t)arctic

4.

(c / s)led

5.

(b / v)olcano

6.

w(i / a)nd

Literacy Center Pronunciation

B. Read and circle the words with the same sounds.

1. mou__th__   teeth   south   there

2. bro__th__er   these   thumb   that

3. _th_ree   this   fifth   thank

C. Read the story on pages 40 and 41. Then match the sentence parts.

1. We live •   • have rain.

2. We have a lot of •   • becomes snow or ice.

3. We don't •   • in the Antarctic.

4. Rain quickly •   • strong winds.

D. Number in order. Then rewrite the summary below.

I live in the Antarctic with my friends.

Come and try ice walks and sledding with us!

We have a lot of snow and ice.

1 **Beginning** ....

2 **Middle** ....

3 **End** ....

A Lion and a Skunk

name:

score:

Words

A. Circle the correct words and match them with the pictures.

p	n	l	j	h	b	h	s	v	a
r	h	s	k	j	p	o	n	x	h
x	v	t	f	o	l	l	o	w	g
w	t	g	a	z	b	e	m	o	f
r	o	a	r	k	q	l	p	o	c
f	v	x	t	m	j	k	l	d	e
d	r	c	h	g	k	a	c	s	d
s	w	n	g	f	c	b	y	z	v
i	o	g	r	a	s	s	a	k	e
n	f	e	r	g	o	a	r	y	t

Literacy Center Grammar

B. Unscramble the words to make the correct sentences.

1. (What / smell! / a / bad) ____________________________

2. (good / What / idea! / a) ____________________________

3. (skunk! / a / smart / What) ____________________________

C. Read the story on pages 44 and 45. Then circle True or False.

1. The lion goes through the river.   True   False

2. The skunk farts and it smells bad.   True   False

Summary with the Retelling Cards

D. Circle the correct words. Then rewrite the summary below.

1. A (happy / hungry) lion follows after a skunk.

2. The skunk goes through tall (grass / woods).

3. The lion follows the skunk into the (hole / tree).

4. The lion (laughs / roars) loudly.

5. The skunk (farts / hides) and the lion runs away.

22

Dinosaurs

name:

score:

Words

A. Unscramble the letters to make the words.

1. 

a / pl / te

----

2. 

ll / i / fr

----

3. 

din / aur / os

----

4. 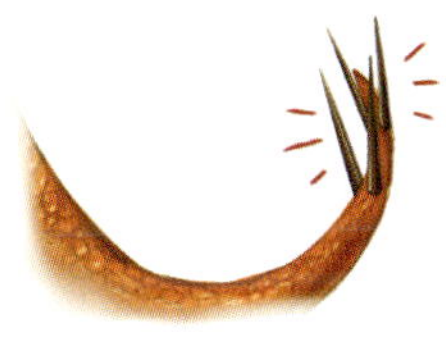

i / sp / ke

----

5. 

w / a / cl

----

6. 

h / n / or

Literacy Center High Frequency Words

B. Write the correct words and read the sentences.

has   its   on

1. They are on ____________________ head.

2. They are ____________________ its tail.

3. Stegosaurus ____________________ many plates.

C. **Read the story on pages 48 and 49. Then circle True or False.**

1. Dinosaurs lived a long time ago. True False

2. Triceratops has three horns on its hands. True False

D. **Write the correct words. Then rewrite the summary below.**

_______________ are all different. Baryonyx has very long _______________. Triceratops has a _______________ and three horns. Stegosaurus has many plates and sharp _______________.

spikes   dinosaurs   frill   claws

Mind Your Manners

name:

score:

Words

A. Fill in the missing letters and rewrite the words.

1. 

a☐ sw☐r

2. 

☐in☐

3. 

do☐n☐oad

4. 

g☐☐e

5. 

d☐nne☐

6. 

ce☐l pho☐e

Literacy Center Pronunciation

B. Read and circle the words with the same sounds.

1. dinn*er*   mann**er**   w**or**k   socc**er**

2. f*ir*st   g**ir**l   b**ir**d   ca**r**d

3. t**ur**n   fa**r**t   h**ur**t   bu**r**ger

C. Read the story on pages 52 and 53. Then match the sentence parts.

1. Allen • • his phone.

2. Allen puts away • • phone rings.

3. Dad's • • your manners.

4. Mind • • downloads some games.

D. Number in order. Then rewrite the summary below.

Allen plays a game at the dinner table. "Mind your manners," says Dad.

Allen gets his first cell phone.

Dad's phone rings and he answers it. "Mind your manners," says Allen.

1 **Beginning** ....

2 **Middle** ....

3 **End** ....

Don't Tease the Monkeys

name:

score:

Words

A. Complete the crossword puzzle.

Literacy Center Grammar

B. Unscramble the words to make the correct sentences.

1. (Don't / the monkeys. / tease) ____________________________________

2. (buy / Don't / ice cream.) ____________________________________

3. (fast food. / eat / Don't) ____________________________________

C. Read the story on pages 56 and 57. Then circle True or False.

1. Alice teases the monkeys.   True   False

2. A monkey takes Ken's ice cream.   True   False

Summary with the Retelling Cards

D. Circle the correct words. Then rewrite the summary below.

1. Ken and Alice (buy / sell) ice cream.

2. They go to see the (monkeys / dinosaurs) at the zoo.

3. "Hey, monkeys! Here is (cotton candy / ice cream)."

4. Ken yells and (listens / teases) the monkeys.

5. Suddenly, a monkey takes Ken's ice cream and (drinks / eats) it.

Polite Words

Words

A. Fill in the missing letters and rewrite the words.

1. 

w ☐ n ☐

----

2. 

☐ ha ☐ k

----

3. 

po ☐ ☐ te

B. Circle the related words.

1. **burp**	leg	mouth	eye
2. **sneeze**	cold	toothache	stomachache
3. **mistake**	happy	proud	sorry

Literacy Center High Frequency Words

C. Write the correct words and read the sentences.

you　　　say　　　when

1. When ___________________ burp, say "Excuse me."

2. ___________________ you want something, say "Please."

3. When someone thanks you, ___________________ "You're welcome."

D. Read the story on pages 60 and 61. Then circle True or False.

1. When you sneeze, say "Thank you."   True   False

2. Polite words make people feel happy.   True   False

Summary with the Retelling Cards

E. Write the correct words. Then rewrite the summary below.

There are some polite words. When you want something, say "______________" When you get it, say "Thank you." When you make a mistake, say "______________" When you burp or sneeze, say "Excuse me." When someone thanks you, say "______________" Then people will be happy.

I am sorry.   You're welcome.   Please.

15 Bird-Watching

Words

A. Choose the correct letters and rewrite the words.

1.

(f / p)ark

2.

b(i / u)rd

3.

(v / w)oodpecker

4.

koo(g / k)aburra

5.

hamm(a / e)r

6.

p(a / e)ck

B. Circle the related words.

1. **bird**　　　　　fly　　　run　　　swim

2. **park**　　　　　food　　place　　time

3. **woodpecker**　　bug　　　fish　　bird

C. **Read the story on pages 66 and 67. Then choose the best answers.**

1. **What is the story about?**

    a. watching birds

    b. singing like a bird

    c. playing with Grandpa

2. **The story happens on __________ .**

    a. Friday afternoon

    b. Saturday afternoon

    c. Sunday morning

3. **Ira, Ed, and Grandpa visit the __________ park.**

    a. sea   **b.** flower   **c.** bird

4. **A woodpecker __________ on the tree.**

    a. eats   **b.** pecks   **c.** jumps

5. **Which bird makes a laughing sound?**

    a.    **b.**    **c.** 

Bird-Watching

name:

score:

Words

A. Circle the correct words and match them with the pictures.

b	c	f	g	l	z	p	a	r	k
i	l	m	b	t	s	f	v	c	o
k	b	t	f	l	y	g	k	w	o
l	v	d	q	k	h	s	t	c	k
r	h	t	b	t	a	p	p	v	a
d	j	b	i	r	m	i	e	b	b
f	z	x	r	i	m	d	c	d	u
w	o	o	d	p	e	c	k	e	r
m	g	p	l	k	r	r	d	y	r
p	r	n	h	r	x	c	z	m	a

B. Circle the related words.

1. **peck**   wing   beak   eye

2. **hammer**   hit   kick   mix

3. **kookaburra**   lion   penguin   woodpecker

C.   Number in order. Then rewrite the summary below.

(   ) Koo koo kakakaka! It sounds like laughing!

(   ) First, Ira, Ed, and Grandpa go to the bird park.

(   ) Then, they see a kookaburra.

(   ) Next, they see a woodpecker.

(   ) Last, Grandpa says, "Let's come here again next week."

(   ) Toc, toc, toc! It sounds like hammering!

Memo

Read & Retell is a three-level reading series for beginner students. This reading program has been designed to strengthen students' foundation of literacy abilities. It particularly focuses on improving students' reading comprehension and oral reading fluency – two skills that are essential for future academic success. Throughout *Read & Retell*, various retelling activities are presented to build students' comprehension proficiency. The series' exciting and captivating oral activities reinforce students' oral reading fluency as well. With *Read & Retell*, students will develop the abilities and habits needed to become fluent readers.

Key Features:

- **Theme-based topics** with engaging fiction and nonfiction stories
- **Basic story elements and reading skills**: characters, time, place, plot, problem & solution, main idea & details
- **Lively Oral Reading Fluency activities** to improve students' reading accuracy, speed, and expression
- **Literacy Center** to boost students' knowledge of pronunciation, grammar, high frequency words, and punctuation
- **Special Sections**: reading day and retelling day
- **Retelling Charts** for special sections
- **Retelling Cards** for each unit

Components:

Student Book / Workbook / Audio CD

Online Resources: www.nebooks.co.kr (Korean) / www.nebuildandgrow.com (English)

Retelling Cards / Teacher's Materials / MP3 Files / Vocabulary Lists / Answer Keys

Read & Retell Series:

<50-60 words>   <60-70 words>   <70-80 words>

Category	Series	Lexile	Components
	Insight Link 1,2,3	500L~610L	Student Book/ Workbook/ MultiROM
	Insight Link 4,5,6	670L~760L	Student Book/ Workbook/ MultiROM
	Subject Link Starter 1,2,3	430L~460L	Student Book/ Workbook/ MultiROM
	Subject Link 1,2,3	520L~610L	Student Book/ Workbook/ Audio CD
	Subject Link 4,5,6	720L~830L	Student Book/ Workbook/ Audio CD
	Subject Link 7,8,9	860L~950L	Student Book/ Workbook/ Audio CD
Listening	Listening Stage Starter 1,2,3		Student Book/ Workbook/ Scripts & Answer Keys/ MultiROM
	Listening Stage 1,2,3		Student Book/ Workbook/ Scripts & Answer Keys/ MultiROM
	Listening Seed 1,2,3		Student Book/ Workbook/ Scripts & Answer Keys/ MP3 CD
	Listening Season 1,2,3 [2nd Edition]		Student Book/ Workbook/ Scripts & Answer Keys/ MultiROM
	Listening Planner 1,2,3		Student Book/ Workbook/ Scripts & Answer Keys/ MP3 CD
Writing	Write Right Beginner 1,2,3		Student Book/ Workbook
	Write Right 1,2,3		Student Book/ Workbook
	Write Right Paragraph to Essay 1,2,3		Student Book/ Workbook
Speaking	Everyone, Speak! Kids 1,2,3		Student Book/ Workbook/ MultiROM
	Everyone, Speak! Beginner 1,2,3		Student Book/ Workbook/ MultiROM
	Everyone, Speak! 1,2,3		Student Book/ Workbook/ MultiROM
Grammar	Grammar Space Kids 1,2,3		Student Book/ Workbook
	Grammar Space Beginner 1,2,3		Student Book/ Workbook
	Grammar Space 1,2,3		Student Book/ Workbook
	Grammar in Mind 1,2,3		Student Book/ Workbook
	Grammar in Focus 1,2,3		Student Book/ Workbook/ Audio CD
	Grammar Effect 1,2,3		Student Book/ Workbook/ Answer Keys